DON'T
HOOK UP

NANCY A. SHENKER & LINDSAY E. BROWN

DON'T HOOK UP

WITH THE DUDE IN THE NEXT CUBE

200+
Career Secrets
for 20-Somethings

This book is dedicated to Lewis Shenker, Nancy's late father,

and Cynthia Sorkin Shenker, Nancy's mother,

and to Cameron Brown and Joan Cunniffe, Lindsay's parents

Distribution by Nancy A. Shenker, nunumedia.com
& Buoy Point Media, buoypoint.com

ISBN 978-0-9827554-2-6

Printed in the United States of America

A Buoy Point Media Production
Editor: Susan Elkin
Copy editor: Laurie Lieb
Cover and interior art: Molly Ostertag
Design and production: Fabia Wargin Design

Buoy Point Media
PO Box 433
Waccabuc, NY 10597
www.buoypoint.com
e-mail: publisher@buoypoint.com

nunu media™
92 Main Street
Suite 100
Yonkers, NY 10701
www.nunumedia.com

Gratitude

Nancy & Lindsay say . . .

Hugs and a huge shout-out to

Lary Rosenblatt and the Buoy Point team . . . you rock!
Fabia Wargin, our designer whose
aesthetic and hard work are appreciated
Susan Elkin, our editor who helped organize our thoughts so well
Laurie Lieb, our copy editor who polished this book to perfection
Molly Ostertag, our young and talented illustrator
who brought our words to life

Nicole Palacino, Nunu graphic designer extraordinaire

Michael Pilla, designer of the awesome cross-gen 2Booms logo

Afshaun Naficy, our reviewer, adviser, and PR idea factory

Sarah Mandell, Sarah Schaffer, Austin George, Laura Willig
and Sarah Birnbaum, our twenty something advisers

Lowell George, the coolest editorial assistant ever

&

All the great girls, women, mentors, and dudes
who supported us throughout our careers
and the creation of this book

Nancy (aka The Boss Lady) Says . . .

This book is dedicated to Lewis, my late father, who always believed in my writing skills and often called me "nunu," the inspiration for my newest venture, nunu media™, a publishing company specializing in pithy, fun, inspirational content.

And special thanks to:

- All my many bosses—men and women—who taught me what I know today (even some of the really bad habits). Jeanne Littas (my first boss out of college), Ed Bolger, Bob McCord, Karen Hochman, Janine Stern, Loren Smith, Steve Cone, James Desrosier, Nick Utton, and Rick White stand out in my mind. And, if I worked for you and didn't give you a call-out, please don't take it personally—remember, it's all business.

- The recruiters who helped me say "Buh-bye" and move on when it was time—Sally of Bert Davis and Pat of the Cheyenne Group. You believed in my talents and helped me rock interviews.

- My girlfriends—Jane, Beth, Sue, Becky, Steph, Helaine, Jo, Cathy, Susan, Barb, the Nancys, Grace, Joan, Kris, Sarah, and the Stacys. You have always shared my successes, my drama, and my whining. And my guy friends, EO/Accelerator buddies, and brothers (Andy and Abe) —who taught me to take body blows and not to always think like a girl.

- The hundreds of wonderful employees and colleagues over the years who helped me become a more reasonable boss lady and professional. Warner Wims deserves a special shout-out.

- My coauthor and partner in crime and writing, Lindsay. Even though you once unfriended me, all is forgiven. I am blessed to have you in my life. You inspire me, calm me, teach me, and give me faith in digital natives.

- My daughters, Austin and Lowell George, who are embarking on their own work journeys now. (And, if you ever slack off or hook up with that cube dude, we need to have a SERIOUS talk!)

- Kenny…we knew and loved each other long before I was "the boss lady" and you were "the boss man."

- And of course, my mom, Cynthia. She had a career and a personal brand before they were even considered cool. And she taught me how to be strong and hold fast to my beliefs.

Lindsay Says . . .

I graduated from college four short years ago and entered the real world scared and overwhelmed like so many recent grads, but driven. Since then, I've learned many lessons the hard way, changed career paths more times than I'd like to admit, and overcome an eating disorder. It's been a rocky road at times, but I struggled and survived, and I owe many people my sincerest thanks.

I'd like to thank my parents, my biggest fans, for their undying love, support, and sacrifice. My father, Cam Brown, taught me how to be courageous and how to get what I want in life—a gift I will never be able to repay. My mother, Joan Cunniffe, encouraged me to pursue my passions, even when they took me across the globe. To Brendan and Kevin, my wiseguy younger brothers, I am very proud of you both and see you headed to great places.

To my devoted family and friends, who have stuck by me and supported me, I thank you all from the bottom of my heart and treasure my relationships with each and every one of you.

I'm indebted to a small and exceptional group of mentors for helping me find my way as a young working girl: Paige Lockwood, Beth McGuire, Randi Luckman, Jerry Cosgrove, Maria Verna, Chris Law, Cathy Hartman, Geri Holton, Michael Aiken, Starre Vartan, and Vanessa Leggard. Paige and Beth, you are the epitome of grace and excellence under pressure. I'm a better businesswoman thanks to you both.

To my favorite boss lady and coauthor, Nancy A. Shenker, your spirit and work ethic inspire me. You're my mentor and friend, and I thank you for cheering me on and pushing me to be better.

And finally, my darling Dan, you are the light of my life.

Contents

PART ONE

OK...Now What the Hell Do I Do With My Life?

Graduating is a huge relief—
no more studying...homework
deadlines...papers to write.
But entering the work world
brings with it a new set
of challenges and stresses.

Suddenly, you're the new kid in the kindergarten class again—not sure what to expect when you stride into your first job in your uncomfortable new shoes—much the way you peered into that classroom many years ago, staring up at that tall stranger and those 25 unfamiliar faces.

Maybe you knew exactly what you wanted to do from the time you were five years old and dressed up your stuffed animals as patients so you could heal them as a famous brain surgeon. But if you're like most recent graduates, you're probably perplexed by all the options in the real world and are embarking on this new path with a combination of excitement, confusion, and total terror.

You'll never land a great job if you come across as timid, anxious, or lost, dazed, and confused. Employers look for people with purpose. And, even if you're not quite there yet, read these tips and learn to practice projecting yourself as the "young woman to watch" (and hire).

Here are the keys to a successful job search:

Confidence: Feeling good about who you are and what you're capable of

Self-honesty: Knowing what you aren't—and being OK with that

Humility: The ability to listen and learn from other people and ask for help

Guts: Willingness to get out there and hustle for what you want (without being a spoiled brat or a bully)

Focus: Having a plan and timeline and staying the course, despite disappointments and distractions

Remember that you're likely to have a career that lasts forty or fifty years, so if you don't pick the right job right out of college you'll have lots of opportunities for do-overs. How you think and feel about what you do is as important as what you actually do every day!

The first part of this book will teach you how to create a compelling personal brand for yourself, face your fears, network better than your peers, and knock any interviewer's socks off. Most graduates don't have a clue what they want to do with the rest of their lives. That's OK. You've spent the past twelve or fifteen years being told what to do and when to do it. If you're lucky, you got to choose lots of electives. But figuring out a career path is like choosing electives without the course catalog. If you don't have the foggiest idea how you're going to earn a living, don't despair. This section can help.

Even if you are lucky enough to have landed a job before graduation or are already on to your next job, be sure to read it anyway. Some of the wisdom applies to day-to-day job survival too!

chapter one

Who Are You?
Personal Branding 101

You know your name, your address (unless you're in the process of moving out of your parents' home), who your friends are, and who you're dating (most of the time). But have you really ever explored who YOU are? What makes you unique? What are your passions and dislikes? What are your core beliefs and values? What types of people inspire and energize you? We'll help you get to know yourself better so you can establish a strong personal brand and articulate to the world, and a prospective employer, who the heck you really are.

1. Dig deep. Yeah, this sounds pretty New-Agey. But taking a look past the mirror and diving deep into your head will help you pave a career path that feels like the right fit for you. Let's pinpoint your passions so you don't wind up doing something that you despise. Answer these questions honestly: What do you get the most satisfaction from doing? What interests you the most? What types of clubs did you join in school? Are you willing to take risks? Where did you choose to go on vacations? Do you like being inside or outside? Moving or sitting still? See what The Boss Lady has to say on the topic.

2. Define your values. To truly build your own brand and stand out among your peers, you have to know what you stand for first. Make a list of attributes and beliefs that you believe identify who you are and what your priorities are.

3. Be true to yourself about what it is that you really want; base your goals and beliefs on your own experiences and what you want out of life. Don't allow peer pressure to sway your career choices.

4. Of course you have to support yourself and money does matter. But happiness has a value too, and a public service or media or teaching career can be personally rewarding and afford you opportunities that sitting in a cubicle might not. Plus, as you move up the ladder, some of these careers can lead to more lucrative options.

> ## DON'T BE A BANKER IF YOU'RE REALLY A POET

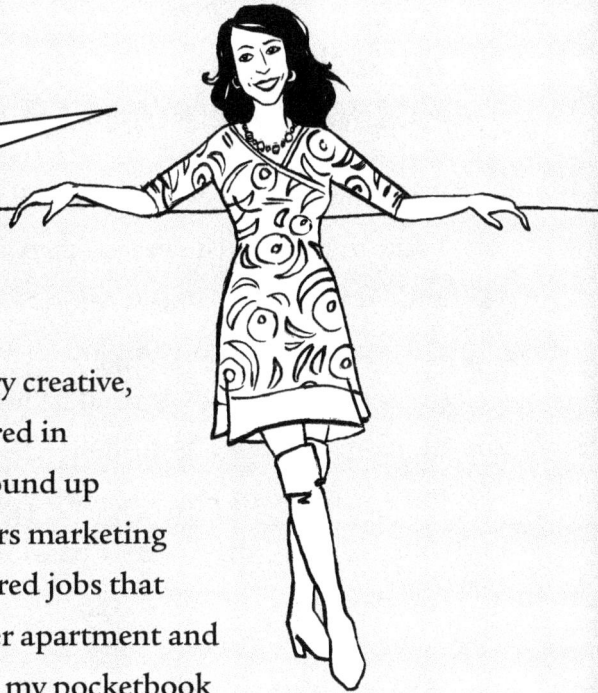

Even though I was always very creative, loved pop culture, and majored in English and psychology, I wound up spending many unhappy years marketing banking products. I was offered jobs that enabled me to move to a nicer apartment and buy better clothes, so I chose my pocketbook over my passion. Of course, a chick has to make a living and I don't regret any of my career decisions because I learned a lot wherever I worked. But once I returned to publishing and started my own businesses, I realized that enjoying what you do every day is as important as that Platinum AmEx card. And, if you can have both, you've hit the career jackpot!

Assessment tests and career counselors can take you only so far with job recommendations. Thousands of jobs exist that you may never have imagined...professional blogger, food stylist, grocery warehouse analyst, mystery shopper, floral designer. Talk to your parents' friends, comb websites like Doostang, and check the careers sections of your favorite sites.

Use the Passion Pinpointer Worksheet as your road map to find the job that is truly the perfect fit!

17

THE BOSS LADY'S
PASSION PINPOINTER WORKSHEET

Write out the answers for the Passion Pinpointer Worksheet. You can fold up the paper, carry it with you, show it to friends and family, add to it as ideas strike you, and refer to it as you go. Once your search is complete, keep it in a safe and special place (underwear drawer? journal?) One day you'll want to refer back to it and see where it ultimately led you. When you're job-hunting again, it will prove useful. You'll probably fine-tune it over time, as you cultivate new passions. And who knows? Perhaps you'll pass it on to your daughters!

1. What activities in life make you the happiest? Do not limit your responses to work or school stuff. If you love ziplining, crocheting, tending to pets, or organizing your closet, put those things down too!

   _____

   _____

   _____

   _____

2. What activities make you miserable?

   _____

   _____

   _____

   _____

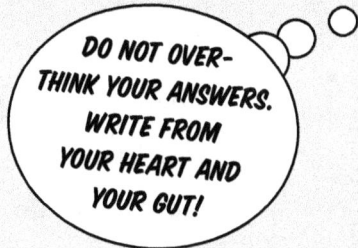

3. What were your favorite school classes? Why?

DO NOT OVER-THINK YOUR ANSWERS. WRITE FROM YOUR HEART AND YOUR GUT!

_____

_____

_____

_____

4. On a scale of 1–5, how much do you like:

__ Meeting new people   __ Writing

__ Spending time alone   __ Math

__ Solving problems   __ Designing
                               or creating things
__ Following direction
   and structure   __ Organizing

__ Leading a group

5. In school, I was usually the girl who _____.

6. If you were stranded on an island, what three things would you bring with you to kill time?

_____

_____

_____

7. Write ten adjectives that you would use to describe yourself. Show the list to friends and relatives and refine it.

_____   _____

_____   _____

_____   _____

_____   _____

_____   _____

19

Then, look at your answers. Do certain themes emerge? Do you like taking risks and working in unstructured environments? Or do you prefer quiet and thoughtful activities in small groups? What really makes you happy? Food? Fashion? Finances? As you consider different paths, evaluate jobs to make sure they contain enough of the stuff you love.

But be realistic and open-minded. Few jobs (especially right out of college) can deliver 100 percent of what you're looking for. Learning new skills and growing as you work are important too.

Self-Doubt Is So Uncool

Self-doubt will sabotage your personal branding efforts so let's work on facing your fears! When you're honest with yourself about what it is that you really want in life, your own negative perceptions and insecurities can creep in and get in your way. "Am I really qualified for that position?" you might ask, talking yourself out of even sending a résumé. Trying anything new and stretching is always going to prompt a certain level of insecurity and uneasiness. But how will you grow into a smart, self-assured, and confident woman if you remain in a bubble and never step outside of it and do something that makes you a little uncomfortable? When you get into that mode of self-doubt, here's how to jump out of it.

5. Catch your fears in the act and recognize when they've gotten the best of you. When fears and negative self-perceptions start creating chaos in your head, write them down on paper. Stare at the paper for a while and then crumple it up and toss it. Farewell, fears! Although acknowledging and trashing your terror and doubt is a good first step, overcoming them is not always that easy. Read on...

6. Create a worst-case scenario list. When fear is speaking louder to you than courage, think about what the worst possible outcomes might be and jot them down. You'll realize that all the bad scenarios you've conjured up aren't so bad at all.

7. Give fear a bear hug. Try doing new things that make you feel scared or uncomfortable. Walk right up to that woman who you've admired for a long time and talk to her, send out that résumé for a job you think you're not qualified for, or try a new class that previously intimidated you at the gym. Remember all the things in your life that you did but were terrified about at first. Learning to drive? Skiing a black diamond? Trying out for the varsity soccer team? Trying a new hairstyle or fashion look? Remind yourself of all the things you thought you couldn't do at first, but ultimately conquered. This will give you a boost of confidence.

8. Know what you want and tune out other people's fearful thoughts or negative "glass half empty" advice. Once you've completed the Passion Pinpointer Worksheet, go for it.

You're the one who will have to wake up every single morning doing the job that you want to do, so your perception is the only "stamp of approval" that you need.

9. If a downer family member or friend tries to arouse fear or negativity in you, telling you why you shouldn't pursue the path that you truly want, tell her to take a hike, nicely! Validate her feelings by listening to what she has to say, but politely and firmly tell her that you "appreciate her advice" but "you're confident your choice is right for you." People often inject their own experiences and insecurities when giving advice to younger people, so try to understand where a person is coming from. Look deeper into why someone might be giving you the sort of advice they're offering. "Is he urging me to get into sales only because he's been successful in it?" "Does she really think I'd make a great teacher or does she simply want me to find something that's more secure in this tough economy?"

THE BOSS LADY SAYS

TALK TO THE PUPPET!

Here's a great trick to help you deal with self-doubt. It sounds totally weird, but it really works. Create a "negative voice" that talks to you. You can even give it a name, like Nasty Nelly or Pissy Pam (and, if you really want to take it to the extreme, you can buy a doll or puppet and talk to it, preferably when you are alone and not at work or out in public!). Pretend that the negative voice is actually saying all the things that you're saying to yourself. Your job is to come up with rebuttals and examples of why those accusations and insults are simply not true. You'll find that taking on the voice of doubt can actually bolster your confidence!

If you're spending more than ten minutes a day talking to the voice of negativity (especially if it involves talking to your puppet friend), you should probably seek out a loving friend, family member, or mental health professional to guide you through your tough times.

chapter two

Rock the Real World

So much of your communication these days is online. But searching for a job and finding success early on in your career will challenge you to be impressive face-to-face as well. Of course, you can use social media to connect with influencers, but you can't hide behind your computer screen! You need to be able to make eye contact, shake hands, converse, network like a pro, and carry on phone conversations that break through candidate clutter.

Social skills and the ability to talk to strangers are critical to your job search. Just as you used your fabulous personality and wit to dazzle that cute guy at the party, you'll be applying your gifts of gab and charm (and resourcefulness) to find the person who's going to hire you, or introduce you to someone who will!

Who Do You Know?

10. Tap into your very own network. The network of people you know will expand in time but even a young woman right out of school has a network, a circle of people you have access to and who can potentially help you.

11. Do some sleuthing to determine if anyone you know—your family, friends, college alumni, and so on—has connections in the field of your dreams. If you have your sights set on a particular organization, the same rules apply. Work those connections! Don't be afraid to ask for what you want. What's the worst thing someone could say to you? No? And if she does, simply ask if she knows someone else who can help you connect to the next person. Ask for an introduction via email on LinkedIn, or suggest that she circulate your résumé or give the human resources department of your dream company "a little ring." Organizations often favor those candidates who were recommended through word of mouth.

12. Join organizations, clubs, and online groups that will introduce you to new people. Sometimes it just takes one encounter to change your world, so create opportunities for yourself.

13. Be approachable. When you attend networking events or meetings but look disengaged because you're playing on your cell phone out of nervousness, you send out a disinterested vibe that could lose you the chance to meet the right people. Limit phone use while you're trying to network and look interested in what's going on and who's there (even if you're not).

Here are examples of networking communities:

- Alumni organizations

- Nonprofits in your field of interest (many are looking for volunteers or youth board members too!)

- LinkedIn groups and local meet-up groups

- Facebook and Google+. They aren't just for uploading photos and posting! Many businesses and causes have established groups. Be sure to clean up your profile and/or use privacy settings if you're using social networking sites for job-hunting or networking.

- Add your own!

Find a Sherpa

Just as a Sherpa helps travelers navigate rocky new terrain and foreign lands, your mentor will help you clear a path throughout your career. (She might even bring along refreshments!) While you're getting your networking on, you should set your sights on selecting your mentor. A mentor is a more experienced person who is working in the field that you are interested in. Since you can have more than one, try to find both female and male mentors as they'll provide you with different perspectives. A mentor should be someone you admire and aspire to be five or ten years from now.

14. Identify the person and reach out to her with a phone call, a note, a LinkedIn request, a direct message on Twitter, or a friend request on Facebook. Be bold and be specific—for example, "I just graduated from college...I admire what you've done... would you be willing to help me get my career off the ground?"

15. If she ignores you or is dismissive, move on. A true mentor really enjoys helping young people succeed.

16. Once you've found that mentor, hold onto her for dear life and nurture the relationship. Set up monthly calls or meetings, and reach out to her for advice and help in making the right decisions along the way.

17. Don't be a mentor leech! Mentorship is not a one-way street; it should be a symbiotic relationship. Even though you're the one who needs guidance, you'll be surprised to learn that you might even inspire your mentor in some ways. Offer to teach an older mentor how to use social media. Or share knowledge of new trends and perspectives from your generation. If your mentor has children, knowing how you're thinking can even be helpful to her as a mother. As your relationship strengthens, a deep friendship can form.

THE BOSS LADY SAYS...

BE LADY GAGA, TIDE, OR A PAIR OF LOUBOUTINS

Alas, in order to compete in today's cluttered job market, you really need to stand out. You're not a rock star, a handy-dandy stain stick, or a trendy shoe label, but the same principles of product branding apply to personal branding as well. Personal branding is simply creating a consistent, compelling, and *credible* persona that will distinguish you from your competition (in this case, other grads who are seeking jobs).

29

We could write an entire book on personal branding dos and don'ts, but for the purposes of this brief section, all you need to know is that when you're presenting yourself to the outside world you should always be memorable, genuine, and unique. (Remember, however, a very fine line exists between self-confidence and narcissism.)

A strong personal brand will define how other people describe you after spending time with you. It's how you want to be viewed by the business world.

Whether you are establishing yourself as the "thoughtful, helpful, articulate, and quiet young woman who is deeply committed to the environment" or the "outgoing blogger who seems to know her way around the fashion world," you need to think carefully about how your behavior, writing, online presence, and, yes, even your choice of attire can reinforce your image to the people who can affect your future.

BE WHO YOU ARE WITHOUT BEING AN EXTREME VERSION OF YOURSELF. THINK:

- Confident, not cocky
- Calm, not catatonic
- Self-assured, not self-absorbed
- Witty, not clownish
- Curious, not interrogating
- Assertive, not pushy

And then make sure that these attributes come through both in your in-person networking and in your social media persona via your behavior, profile, posts, and tweets. You want to be memorable for all the right reasons.

chapter three

Social (Media) Status

Imagine landing a great job only to get called into HR just a few weeks later because of something you said on Facebook. How you present yourself online is more important now than ever before. And your "conduct"—your status, photos, and so on—is a big part of your personal brand and says a ton about you.

18. Even if public relations isn't your strong suit, think of yourself as your very own publicist as you manage your web presence. Just as PR pros think through every single word and image associated with their clients, you too need to ensure that your online identity is consistent with your personal brand (that is, how you want to be perceived by the world). Every post, tweet, and image you share is as important as your actions and the clothes you wear.

Clean It Up

19. Google yourself before someone else does. Search your name often or set up a Google Alert. If you find something inappropriate, take fast action. Facebook posts can be removed and you can ask friends or family members to kindly take down "bad stuff."

20. Remove the racy photos, like the shot of you as a sexy librarian at a Halloween party or one of you dancing in a bikini during spring break. Use your better judgment and get rid of any photos of yourself that could be deemed inappropriate by an employer.

21. Assess your relationship with every single person on each of your social networking sites. Everyone you allow into your online world has some sort of access to your life, so use discretion when adding "friends," particularly new colleagues.

22. Keep good company online. If people are using your space to behave inappropriately or hijacking your feed with negativity, it's OK to unfriend them.

23. Use privacy settings to control what and how much you share. When adding colleagues or new friends to Facebook, manage their access to your profile. You may decide to give your real friends full access to your profile while filtering your colleagues' ability to view your wall or photos. But beware: Companies develop clever ways to gain access to prospective and current employees' profiles, even if you think it's on "lock down" with privacy settings.

Watch Your Language, Missy!

Your words on the Internet have the power to make or break your online branding efforts, too. Whether you're commenting on an online article or photo, tweeting, blogging, or posting away, you must always keep in mind that anyone with a computer can read anything you type.

24. Foul language and misspelled words should be avoided at all times. You'd think that this would be a no-brainer, but you'd be surprised by how many well-educated young women carelessly publish expletives and typos. Think about it from an employer's perspective: If you looked into a job candidate and discovered a Facebook post filled with typos and curses, would you want that person working for you?

25. Read over anything you choose to share three times before publishing.

26. Don't incorporate "text speak" into your online communication. It looks childish and completely unprofessional. Unless you're in middle school or you're using Twitter (which has a character limit), avoid slang and unnecessary abbreviations.

27. Be mindful of what and how much you choose to share online. Verbal diarrhea online is more than unattractive; it's a complete waste of time. A little mystery can help your personal brand and set you apart from your TMI posting peers, encouraging people to get to know you better in the real world.

28. Some things are better left unsaid. If you're pissed off about a situation and have the urge to rant and rave, go meditate or hit the gym instead. Power branders don't share their issues with the world.

29. Align all of your online communication and the content you share with positivity. The good energy and intention behind each post or tweet you share can be felt throughout the online world. Do away with any negativity and start making people feel good with uplifting, smile-inducing content!

THE BOSS LADY SAYS

HERE'S YOUR SOCIAL MEDIA HOMEWORK

Sorry, girls. You may have thought you were all done with after-hours assignments. But this Boss Lady has a few more tasks for you to wrap up before you can get an A+ in career management and job hunting.

Social media, if done right, can be super-powerful in your job search and personal branding. Your "Google cred" is as important as the first impression you make in the real world.

So here are five simple ways you can use social media to help you get hired:

- Post an online résumé, using one of the free blogging apps like WordPress.

- Buy the URL for your name (e.g., www.nancyashenker.com) and get a tech-savvy friend to point it to your online résumé.

- Learn to use LinkedIn. It's where the power professionals hang out. Twitter can also be a great self-promotion and connecting tool. Direct-message people you want to meet or retweet something interesting they tweeted. (Just don't do it so often that you come across as a suck-up or creeper.)

- Set up a separate Facebook page for your "professional self" and friend brands, and individuals, in your field of interest.

- Start a blog or comment on other people's blogs in your "passion category." Listing your own blog on your résumé shows your hiring manager or boss you have initiative (and that you can write too).

Check our website (www.2booms.com) for our "Get Social … Get Ahead" webinar and workshop schedule. And go to the head of the career class!

Pitching Yourself

Once you've rebranded yourself, you need to head out there and look for a job. So, before moving on to Chapter 4, consider the dos and the don'ts of a successful job search. Admittedly, a job hunt can be overwhelming—especially for a newbie like you. But remember, you've done this before. Applying to colleges was also a daunting process and you handled that. Job hunting isn't much different from college hunting. With both you must be well-prepared and patient, do your research and exude your personal best in public. Except this time around, you're the one that will eventually get paid!

30. Look for a position in fields that you're passionate about. Keep your Passion Pinpointer Worksheet by your side during this process.

31. Turn looking for a job into a job itself. As with any job, give it your all because you will get what you put into your job search. Set aside certain hours each day. Get dressed as if you are going to work each day...job-hunting in your PJs can lead to frequent napping or TV-watching.

32. Open your eyes and ears. Thousands of wonderful and varied jobs are out there. Like shoes, sometimes you have to experiment with various styles until you find "the best job." Sometimes a career path is a winding one.

33. Connect with as many people as you possibly can! Job-hunting is a numbers game: the more people you meet, the more opportunities you'll create for yourself.

34. Develop an "elevator pitch" that sums up who you are and what you want to do in thirty seconds or less. Memorize it and when you find yourself meeting someone new, you'll be able to express yourself quickly and articulate what you're looking for.

35. Don't turn up your nose at any opportunity. Some great jobs are unpublished, and employers will sometimes create a job for the right candidate.

chapter four

Study Up and Show Up:
Ideal Interviewing

Lots of sources can provide interviewing strategies and tips and we don't claim to be experts. But here are just a handful of our fave tips from our own experiences (as both interviewee and The Boss Lady who makes the decisions).

36. Once you get the interview, the next step is to prepare for it so you feel confident rather than anxiety-ridden. Even one critical blunder can disqualify you from the running, especially if you're one of hundreds of candidates.

37. Know thy interviewer. You didn't walk into an exam in college without studying, thinking you were going to ace it, did you? The same principles apply to interviewing. If you want to "give great interview," you have to hit the books hard and study up.

38. Carefully review the website of the organization and have a solid understanding of what it does. Google and investigate the people that you know you'll be meeting with too. Bios on the company's site, LinkedIn, and Facebook profiles are a great place to start. Read any articles that the company or interviewer has been featured in and carefully research any recent press developments and trends in the industry—all of which will make for great talking points.

39. Practice makes perfect. Anticipate questions and then have some fun and role-play. What that means is that you should create a list of frequently asked interview questions and practice responding aloud to yourself or with a family member or friend.

40. Prepare questions to ask your interviewer. Prospective employers will surely ask if you have any questions for them at the end of your interview. Dead silence is awkward and off-putting. Asking good questions shows that you're enthusiastic, proactive, and interested in the business. Unlike what your grade school teacher told you, there **are** such things as stupid questions in the working world, so you'll want to think ahead. Line up about five questions to ask your interviewer. It's even OK to write them down on a note card (your interviewer will know you've been thinking). If you haven't been asked for questions and the interview is coming to an end, say, "Would you mind if I asked you a few questions about the position (or company)?" It would be a shame to let those great questions go to waste!

41. Even a "bad" interview can have a good result. Each opportunity to talk to a stranger and show your stuff is practice for the next time.

Seal the Deal

42. Dress for the job you want. While you're doing your pre-interview research, try to get a feel for the company's culture to help you determine an appropriate outfit. When unsure, err on the side of caution and dress conservatively.

43. Be early and well-rested. A day or two prior to the big day, figure out exactly how long it should take you to get to your interview and plan to arrive fifteen minutes early. Give yourself some cushion for traffic or subway delays. Arriving thirty minutes early is better than even one minute late. Hit the sheets at a respectable time so you'll be fresh and alert for the day of your interview.

44. Be sure to bring along an extra copy of your résumé. It makes life easier for the person you're meeting with.

45. Exude confidence. Even if you're shaking in the knees and have hives on your chest, maintain eye contact with your interviewer and give anyone you meet a firm handshake (if you swoop down from above your grip will be a bit firmer...but don't crush bones as you squeeze).

46. Ask for a business card; then say, "Thanks." You'll be a bit nervous and anxious to exit, but before you do so, make sure you have the information you need. Then ask when you should expect to hear from the company. Good businesses take the hiring process seriously, and sometimes the decision takes time. Knowing when you should expect to hear from them will alleviate any post-interview anxiety.

47. Later that day, when you're back home and in your sweats, send a brief thank-you note. The next day is too late. Personal hand-written notes make a huge impression. You can send one as well as an email. The more thanks, the merrier!

THE BOSS LADY SAYS

TRUTH OR DARE

Yeah, we older folk can be pretty resourceful when using social media and snooping around in the real world too. So if you have a dark shadow or gap in your past, you're better off coming clean and explaining before your dirty little secret is discovered.

For example, if you took a year off from college because you partied too hard and flunked out, own up to it and reinforce the positives of how the experience ultimately helped you and how you grew as a result. ("I fell into the wrong crowd, made some stupid choices, and exercised bad judgment when I was younger. But when I went back to school, I was much better prepared and in fact I wound up getting great grades and even mentoring other kids during my job as a camp counselor. Learning from my mistakes was an important step for me.") Note that by making reference to a job you successfully held, you are proving you are a safe bet as a hire.

Do not blame other people or external circumstances for your errors. Resist the urge to divulge too much information online and in job interviews. Unless you've committed a violent crime or done something truly heinous, most decent bosses will forgive youthful mistakes. But flat-out lying is never a good idea.

They Want You! But Do You Want Them?

The time will come when you'll receive a job offer, and it will be a gratifying feeling. But don't get cocky and spike the football in the end zone. You still have work to do. You're now faced with the decision of either accepting the offer or rejecting it. Whichever way you sway, there's a way to handle the decision well.

48. Play it cool. Whether you received the offer via phone call or email, respond quickly but don't blurt out a decision immediately. Express enthusiastically how wonderful the news is, and then ask the person who offered you the job if you may have a few days to think about the decision.

49. Even If you know right away you'd like to accept (because you're eager to leave your current job, sick of being broke, or tired of living at home with your parents), don't freak out with excitement and scream "YES!" on the phone. Pull yourself together, take a deep breath, and then accept the offer the next day.

50. Respond on your employer's terms. The person you've been communicating with should inform you when he needs your decision. You should respect that time frame as well as the person who offered you the job. If he says he needs your decision in three days, that's your deadline.

51. Never burn bridges. After some deliberation, if you decide the job just isn't right for you, call the organization soon and respond courteously. Then, send a letter expressing thanks for the offer and explaining that the position isn't the right fit for you. Wish the company the very best and be sure to send your note declining the offer within the requested time frame. It's a small world and that hiring manager you dissed could move to a different company and wind up running the show at the next place you want to work for. If you burned her, she'll burn you down the road when your paths cross. Walk away from the situation with courage, class, and professionalism.

52. If you want the job, stay on your pretty, pedicured toes. When you've decided to accept an offer (woo hoo!), be sure you relay your gratitude and excitement about the position. No need to send a novel about how thrilled you are. You expressed enthusiasm during your interviews.

53. Submit any paperwork such as the actual acceptance letter or necessary documents on time and in the way in which the company requested, whether it be email, snail mail, or fax. Proofread... proofread... proofread.

54. Respond to anyone from the organization in a timely fashion too. Any delays could send the message that you're pursuing other opportunities, causing the company to relaunch its interview process. Remember that it's not a done deal until documents are signed, so even though you've been offered the job, if you act a fool at the end, the offer could be rescinded. Then you'd be back to square one, depressed and desperate and on the prowl.

I HAVE SEEN IT ALL!
CANDIDATE HEAVEN
AND INTERVIEW HELL

As I think back on the hundreds of interviews I've conducted and the good, the bad, and the ugly, I reflect on great examples and some of the immediate turn-offs (some of them humorous).

Here are some best practices, based on what dream candidates do to get job offers.

- Send a killer cover note* with your résumé and follow up with a phone call.

- If an ad says "no attachments," pay attention. Follow instructions to the letter.

- Begin your note with a proper salutation, using a name, not "Hey!" or "Dear Sir." (A woman might be reading your note.)

- Make sure your note is 100 percent typo-free. (Remember, spell-check doesn't catch everything. Reread your note out loud before you send!)

- Do your homework. Rather than simply regurgitating what's on a company website or in an ad, talk about why you'd be a good fit.

- Be flexible about scheduling a time to meet. Do not be a date-setting diva. If you really want a job, you'll figure out a way to work around the interviewer's schedule.

- Come clean about gaps in your education or work history and allow the interviewer to speak to references who can shed light on your true character and choices. Do not be defensive or cocky.

- Don't try to fake it. If you don't know something the interviewer asks about, admit it.

- Exhibit persistence and patience. Follow up to show interest, but don't phone-stalk the interviewer.

- If you don't get a job offer, be gracious. Leaving a good impression always pays off in the long run.

*A killer cover note is enthusiastic, specific, and just the right combination of selling your skills without bragging or being pompous. It tells the reader exactly what you can bring to the company. But be realistic. No one will believe that a recent grad can really solve all a company's problems.

SAGE ADVICE AND HORROR STORIES

The following are all based on true stories of interviews I have lived through. Be forewarned...

- Do not show up late without calling. If you think you're going to be late due to unforeseen circumstances, call as soon as you can, explain the situation, apologize, and ask if rescheduling is preferable to a late meeting. One candidate called several times to update me on the status of his car problems. Not relevant, unless you happen to be a garage mechanic.

- Do not adjust your undergarments or engage in other personal grooming during an interview, no matter how nervous you may be. One woman stood up mid-sentence, reached under her skirt to adjust her slip, and sat back down without missing a beat. Tidy, but weird.

- Do not ask about money within the first few minutes of the interview.

- Do not complain bitterly about previous jobs and bosses. Employers are skittish about anyone who trash-talks... how do they know they won't be next?

- Do not hug the interviewer goodbye. Yes, I have been hugged. But never kissed.

- Do not insist on showing a portfolio of work. Mention that you brought it and, if the interviewer wants to see it, she will ask. One candidate asked me about five times if he could show me his samples. The job did not involve writing or creative development, so the materials weren't particularly relevant to the situation at hand.

- Do not handle things on the interviewer's desk. I have a fairly expensive crystal globe on my desk, and whenever anyone picks it up and plays with it, I cringe. It's not a baseball. And, even if it were, I would feel a bit violated.

- Do not reveal personal details, health issues, or family drama. Overcoming hardships can make you appear more resilient, but stay general. TMI is still too much information—especially when meeting a relative stranger.

- Do not be extremely rigid about salary requirements. Turning up your nose just because of money can be a mistake, especially if what you want and what's being offered are pretty close. Instead, negotiate a review after three months or a performance-based bonus. After you gain more work experience, you can drive a harder bargain.

- Do not overstay your welcome. When the interviewer says good-bye, it's time to leave.

If something truly humiliating or awful happens during an interview, do not give up! I once interviewed someone who sweated so profusely during our conversation that the table had to be wiped down afterward. He simply apologized at the end of our meeting and said that he tends to perspire vigorously when nervous. He ended up getting the job and we still joke about it years later. I valued his humor and honesty.

PART TWO

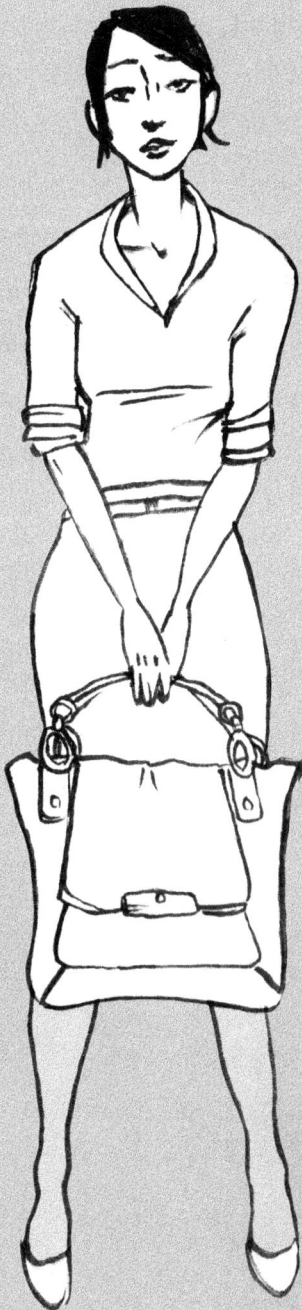

I Got The Job! Now What?

Landing your very first job and
even the first big "bump-up"
after that one is a huge deal.

On-the-Job Behavior

After soul-searching, networking, and revamping your personal brand, you rocked rounds of interviews and now here you are—on the payroll! We're so proud.

Or maybe you're just starting the job search, in college and hoping to get ahead (you little go-getter, you), or you're a young pro looking to brush up on your on-the-job behavior. Perhaps you recently got into a nasty battle with a colleague and decided you ought to develop better work manners. Wherever you are in your career, keep on reading, because the next section is filled with everything you need to

know about handling yourself on the job—from a courtroom or class-room to a cube or Congress. Most of the tools and tactics we share can be applied to relationships and situations outside of work, too! Check out www.2booms.com for some of our other fave resources on office behavior.

Getting a college or graduate degree is an impressive feat, but mastering the art of handling yourself well in any situation on the job might feel like uncharted waters for you. You can rattle off books and information on the subjects you studied like an expert, but when it comes to dealing with the at-work cattiness and complexi-ties of your new workplace menagerie, you may feel completely lost and frustrated.

Your work environment—the place where you'll spend a huge chunk of your time—will present its challenges, but when you know how to handle yourself well, a whole new world of opportunities will open up for you. The following chapters will inspire and teach you how to be your very best at work on a daily basis.

chapter five

WELCOME
NEW
HIRES!

The First Days (or Daze?)

Even if your interview experience
was pure rapture, your first few days
and weeks at a new job can leave you
feeling confused, depressed,
ignorant, pissed-off,
or even terrified. Give it time!
You are starting something new and foreign.
Only time, effort, and relationship-building can turn
this strange place into your new home.

55. Make sure you know where you're going and how to dress on your first day. It seems obvious, but a confirming call to your boss before you start will begin the process of relationship-building and show you take your job seriously. Plus, you won't wind up in the wrong place or wearing a suit and pantyhose when the entire team is dressed in jeans and tees.

56. Pack a notebook and pen and write down the names of the people you meet, things that seem important, and even directions to important places like the ladies' room and cafeteria.

57. Speaking of food, pack a light, nonperishable snack. If you don't get asked to a welcome lunch, you won't starve to death!

58. Schedule time to meet with your boss if she hasn't already arranged for it.

59. Expect to be bored and underutilized at first. Unless your employer has a formal training program or the person who had your job before is still there, you might have a bit of downtime while the organization gets used to having you around.

60. If your lull goes on too long, be sure to speak up. Ask your boss what else you can do or read or who else you can meet. Do not use quiet time for personal emails and phone calls or socializing.

FIRST IMPRESSIONS CAN BE LASTING

Research says that lasting impressions are formed by both employers and employees within the first couple of days on the job. It certainly does go both ways. At one job, I was left sitting in the reception area for ninety minutes when I arrived for my first day—despite repeated requests for help. I remember the incident more than ten years later.

How you present yourself to your boss and colleagues during those first days can also leave a lasting impression. Be your best self during those first ninety days (and hopefully beyond).

- Show up on time and don't leave until your boss says it's OK or she leaves. If you're unclear and the hour is getting late, simply ask.

- Dress appropriately (see our tips).

- Smile a lot.

- Go beyond what's expected of you.

- Do not get sucked into a "bad crowd" of gossips, haters, and time-wasters.

- Meet as often as you can with your boss and coworkers and make every effort to come up the learning curve quickly.

- Ask lots of questions and read as much as you can to become familiar with the company and job.

chapter six

Competent Communication

Your ability to communicate effectively at work is vital to your work existence. You're often judged by higher-ups on how you speak, what you say, and how you interact with them and your peers. We've all met people who we knew were intelligent and gifted, yet lacked the ability to connect with others. Their emails seem abrasive and they often have trouble making eye contact when speaking.

On the other hand, you may have encountered someone who is a born "people person." Her conversational skills seem effortless and full of charm. Her email exchanges are respectful, full of purpose, and well conceived. Remember that this positive image is something that can be cultivated and learned. Even the shyest of girls can morph into a socially adept employee. It's not a gift bestowed on a few, but rather a talent that can be acquired with some practice.

In our tech-crazed world, you have endless ways to "talk"—texts, emails, teleconferencing, IM, and phone. Communication at work is more convoluted than ever. Plenty of room for error exists for a young professional. Take the time to learn communication skills and avoid pitfalls that may derail you from your path to success.

Choose Your Words Wisely

61. Cleanse your communication. Brevity is appreciated in the working world because people value their time. So you need to work on removing unnecessary words and ideas. Communications frills and fluff make messages complex and confusing. Your colleagues or clients will spend precious time deciphering what the heck you're actually trying to say! Save the flowery calls, emails, and chats for your girlfriends who may eat your words up. Over time, your leaner word diet will become second nature to you.

62. Stop talking girly-talk. In business communication, be direct. Being forthright about what you're saying or asking for doesn't sound bitchy; it sounds like you know what you want. Don't worry about being terse. When you're communicating with someone, think to yourself: Will this person understand exactly what I mean or what I'm asking for? Direct does not mean rude. Use "please" and "thank you," and use the proper salutations and sign-offs in your emails.

63. Strike "squishy" words from your communications (e.g., use "I believe" or "I think," not "I feel").

64. Think before you type or speak. In the heat of the moment, your thoughtless comments or remarks could get you into real trouble. Give yourself time to weigh out how your words might be perceived by the recipient. This will avoid the hassle of any misunderstandings or saying something you might regret later. Pausing (minutes, hours, or even a day or two) before responding to anything indicates thoughtfulness. Do not be ashamed to ask a colleague for some time to reply.

65. When you're tempted to gossip or trash someone, think long and hard first. Here are a few questions to ask yourself: Might my words offend this person? Am I overstepping my boundaries? Did anyone actually ask for my opinion? How would I feel if she did it to me? And, please, no cursing in the workplace.

Marvelous Meetings

66. Listen more and hush your glossed lips. You'll always stay ahead of your self-promoting peers by simply listening more than you talk. This is an especially valuable skill for a rookie in the workforce because you need to soak up as much knowledge as you possibly can! You don't seriously think you know everything, do you? Encourage others to speak by asking intelligent questions. No one is ever impressed by a know-it-all girl who runs her mouth. And when someone else has the floor, avoid the temptation to check your cell or other personal devices. Give others your undivided attention and let them know you care about what they have to say.

67. When it's your time to shine, speak up! Silence is not golden when it goes on for too long. When you know your stuff or your boss asks for your opinion, use that chance to exude confidence, intelligence, and thoughtfulness.

Before You Press Send . . .

68. You may have more time to chew on what you're going to say in an email, but typing out your brilliant thoughts raises an entirely different set of issues! Proper email etiquette will steer you clear of uncomfortable situations—that dreaded "uh-oh."

69. Many organizations have an email policy, so you'll want to make sure you're up to speed with it. If your company requires an email disclaimer, be sure it's on all of your external and internal communication, as it protects your company from liability.

70. Don't enter the recipient's address before you've finished an email. This can be disastrous, so get into the habit of adding the addressees as the final step before pressing Send. The last thing you want is to accidentally send internal communication to a client or send an email to a colleague who's discussed in the message. One little "oops" after you click Send could be career catastrophe!

71. Read your emails three times before pressing Send to avoid spelling and grammatical errors. Even if you won your third-grade spelling bee, be sure to keep spell-check on so that any misspelled words are flagged. We all make errors from time to time, so swallow your pride and turn that setting on. Check your signature too! Spelling your title or address wrong can happen.

72. Don't be annoying. WHEN YOU WRITE IN CAPITALS IT READS AS IF YOU'RE SHOUTING. Keep the caps lock off. Abbreviations and emoticons are amateur and inappropriate in the working world, so keep LOL, BTW, and :) out of your business emails.

73. Finesse the final touches. Select a meaningful subject line that sums up the purpose of the email in four words or fewer. This is a great place to practice leaving out superfluous and irrelevant words! You should usually begin an email with "Dear XXX." Once you've established a relationship, "Hi, XXX" becomes acceptable. Close your email with an appropriate sign-off such as "Best" or "Regards." Reserve "Much love," "Mwah," or "Peace" for your girlfriends and your honey. If you own your own company one day, you can mandate that your employees close their emails with "Hugs" if that fits with your brand. Until then, play it safe and keep it professional. Use only a work email address for business communications. If you work from home, be sure you know how to use your company's remote access capabilities (including those from your personal devices).

Up Close and Personal

Whether you're sitting around a conference table, a lunch table, or a Skype session, the ability to connect "live" is still an important aspect of business today. Notice how the celebrities, politicians, and business figures you respect all have cultivated their "people presence."

You can develop the power to light up a room when you walk in and to put anyone at ease with your speech. Even in your twenties, you can command respect and attention from your colleagues by the way in which you conduct yourself when speaking face-to-face.

74. Get pumped up! When you meet someone or greet her, be enthusiastic and pair the warm hello with a solid handshake and big smile.

75. Maintain eye contact. That doesn't mean you should creepily stare at someone, but do your best to look someone in the eyes while speaking to her. If you look away, down, or to the side, it sends out a red flag that you're not confident or engaged.

76. When you're speaking to a group, look around at the people you're talking to; don't focus just on one person. Find people who are nodding and smiling and use them as your confidence-boosters.

77. Try your best to remember names correctly! One of the best ways to make a favorable first impression—and to get ahead socially and/or in business—is to retain people's names and use them in conversation. When you first meet someone, say her name three times in your head to help you with retention.

78. If you forget a name, simply fess up. ("I'm so sorry...I know we've met but I've met so many new people here. If you give me your name again, I promise I'll remember!") Then, when she walks away, create a "note" on your phone and quickly type in the name.

BE PHONE-Y
(AND PRACTICE PENMANSHIP)

Back in my day, we didn't have iPhones and keyboards (other than pianos). The only way we could communicate was by telephone (the rotary kind), manual typewriters, and handwritten notes.

Especially when dealing with boomers (folks like me, born before the Internet era), a personal phone call or note on nice professional stationery is a great way to get closer to someone and show her you can speak her language too.

Sometimes the old-fashioned "personal touch" can help a lot:

- A thank-you call or note following an interview

- A request for a meeting

- An apology (when you're late for work or screwed something up)

- An urgent question. All too often people will say, "Well, I sent you an email" when a time-sensitive issue needed attention. I get 300+ emails a day. A phone call is a surefire "clutter buster" and cry for help!

And remember, the phone and handwriting have no spell-check or backspace. So plan your communication in advance. If you're making a tough phone call, make note cards for yourself (but don't sound like you're reading a script). If you send someone a handwritten note, make sure your spelling is correct and your handwriting is legible.

chapter seven

Behave Yourself!
How to Be a Good Girl at Work

You reap what you sow in the workplace, and every action you take has some sort of good or bad consequence. In the moment, some things may seem like a good idea: making out with the dude from the next cube in the supply closet, wearing a sexy skirt to the office, or having a shot of Patrón at lunch on a Friday. Sooner or later, bad behavior will catch up with you. Call it karma, but developing good-girl habits at work will keep you out of trouble and fast-track your career.

"Oh No She Didn't!"

79. First and foremost, read your employer's policy guidelines. Yeah, boring!! But it's like insisting on a condom for your career. Prevention of problems is preferable to an infection that affects your future. It's a gross analogy, but an accurate one. Just one mistake can cost you a great promotion or job. Almost all companies and organizations maintain some sort of employee handbook.

80. Never discuss or tell jokes about politics, religion, sex, race, or sexual orientation at work. Your off-color remark could deeply offend someone and can be cause for firing.

81. Abstain from forwarding questionable emails or YouTube videos too. You didn't write or produce them, but by forwarding them, you're endorsing them.

82. Be a professional, not a skank. Unless you work at Hooters or are a stripper or bartender, you shouldn't show cleavage at work, tempting as it may be. The image that you present to your coworkers and clients should reflect professionalism, so save the short skirts, push-up bras, and low-cut tops for a night out on the town. You want your colleagues and superiors to take you seriously, not look at you as a piece of meat or the subject of catty whispers. Learn to "layer." You can cover up that after-work cami with a sensible cardigan and then disrobe after hours.

83. Every workplace has a different dress code, so look to other young professionals as models for the proper attire. You don't necessarily have to sacrifice your own personal style, but you do have to be respectful of your employer's culture. If you're unsure of whether it's a casual day, it's safest to dress as you typically would.

84. Using a light scent is OK, but be "scent-sible" when applying fragrance. Makeup should be suitable for office lights, not the circus.

85. In general, don't comment on coworkers' appearances. It could get you in all sorts of trouble for harassment. Yes, female employees can be guilty of this too!

86. Do not be a space invader. Respect your coworkers' personal space by not entering their offices, cubes, or desk areas unless invited. Just because you work in spaces without doors doesn't mean you're free to roam. Even a small cube or desk is someone's personal space to work. If you can tell what someone had for lunch when you're speaking to him, you're probably way too close. Take a step back.

87. Once you're speaking with someone, don't overstay your welcome. After you've accomplished what you set out to, get up and say, "I'll let you get back to work."

Office Decor: The Window into Your Soul

88. Your office space (even if it's part of a cube farm, measures four by four, and has no windows) can be as defining as your wardrobe and speech. Make it part of your personal and professional brand.

89. Keep your desktop clean and well-organized. If you appear a slob, you will be perceived as one by your management and peers. Doritos crumbs and used tissues are *not* desk accessories.

90. Choose a few meaningful personal items for your desk decor. They will give coworkers a richer sense of who you are. But avoid the temptation to display your "I love James Franco" or "Hello Kitty" collection. That kind of stuff is best reserved for inside high school lockers, the privacy of a dorm room closet, or a secret place on Facebook.

91. Clean up your desk each night before leaving work (and make your to-accomplish list for the next day). You'll start each day feeling fresh and in control.

Private? Hell No!

92. If you use your computer at work for "personal stuff," think again. "Personal" does not apply at work. If you type something on your office computer you might as well print it out and hand it to your boss. Even if it's on your own Gmail account, you're doing it on work hours on work equipment. Private now = public later!

93. Do not say anything in the office that you couldn't announce in a corporate boardroom. You may be whispering in the cafeteria or ladies' room, but you can never be sure who's around the corner or in the next stall. Better to zip it and save your secrets for your closest girlfriends after work.

THE BOSS LADY SAYS

CLOTHES CALL: WHAT DOES "DRESS FOR SUCCESS" REALLY MEAN?

When I started my career, nude-colored pantyhose were mandatory, even in ninety-degree weather. Open-toed shoes were forbidden in the workplace. And breasts were flattened and hidden. We never had casual Fridays. It was a repressive and often uncomfortable era. (And yet people could smoke cigarettes in their offices, so go figure!)

Office dress codes are ambiguous and vary widely these days, even by industry. Nose rings, orange hair, and tats may be acceptable if you're working in the music industry, but could put you on the no-fly list for career advancement in the financial world.

75

When in doubt, ask! Most women managers will be flattered if a young professional asks for career advice—even if it relates to fashion.

DO AS I SAY, NOT AS I DO

Don't assume that you can just copy the style of the woman in the big corner office. As elitist as it may seem, senior executive women have earned the right to be independent in their choices. Just because your mentor wears blue toenail polish and four-inch, sparkly heels, you shouldn't assume they're part of the universal dress code. When you're a VP, CEO, or other heavy hitter, you get certain rights and privileges.

TEN QUESTIONABLE WORKPLACE STYLES

1. Visible piercings
2. Strange hairdos and hair colors (the definition of "strange," of course, is somewhat subjective)
3. Shorts, leggings, and other booty-revealing bottoms
4. Peek-a-boo underthings
5. Flip-flops
6. Very long nails and exotic nail art
7. Glittery clothes, hair, and makeup
8. Anything that can be mistaken for PJs or underwear
9. Hats (unless you are in the military or police force)
10. Jeans in many businesses (unless you are a farmer or it's casual Friday)

Office Romance or Just Sex?

Sure you might work with a hottie or encounter one at some point who is charming, smart, and helpful. And you might find that you really click with him, or her, in meetings and at drinks after work. And you'll have so much in common (after all, you work for the same company!). A little fling would be superconvenient—you could see your sweetie every day without making plans in advance. Plus...there can be something sneaky about an office romance that adds thrill and excitement to what would be an otherwise ordinary work day.

Sounds pretty tempting, eh? Before you take it from the conference room to the bedroom, know what you're getting yourself into.

94. Think about this...everyone at work is bound to know. Even if you think you're being really discreet, office gossip spreads faster than butter on a warm bagel. People love a juicy love (or sex) story to whisper about.

95. "So what if everyone knows?" you might think. But besides being the subject of office gossip, an office fling is most likely against office policy, believe it or not. Check your employee handbook, because it will be in fine print somewhere in there. What constitutes a "fling"? You can usually assume that any interaction beyond a handshake qualifies as something intimate. How silly would you feel if you lost a really great job because of one terrific (or maybe not-so-terrific) night?

96. That said, if the night is not so good, or you wake up with a killer hangover regretting the decision, how awkward will it be at work the next day? And the day after that…and the day after that!

97. Even if you believe you will have a wonderful relationship, how might it affect your opportunities within the company in the long term? If you break up, how will that feel each day? What if he then starts hooking up with someone else at work? It's one thing to break up with a guy and then watch his new exploits or love unfold on Facebook. It's another thing to witness it in the hallway.

THE BOSS LADY SAYS

YEAH, I WAS YOUNG ONCE, TOO.

And did I always follow this advice? Hell no! But, as the boss, what bothers me most about an office hook-up is the dishonesty. Everyone in the office knows it's going on, but the people involved deny it because they think denial will help them in some way. Best to come clean as soon as you're asked. No need to divulge personal details. I once worked with a woman who had hooked up with our boss. Everyone in the entire company knew and the couple simply fueled our gossip by their attempt at secrecy.

Work Your Work Ethic

Unless you're a Kardashian or a Trump, nothing is going to be handed to you on a silver platter. A strong work ethic is essential if you really want to go anywhere in your career; it's what differentiates the slackers from the superstars.

98. Go-getter girls finish first. Proactive acts will be appreciated by your colleagues and your boss. No matter what industry you're in, take the initiative and anticipate tasks that need to be completed. Even though you'll certainly need guidance from your boss, show her you're an independent thinker and smart woman. If you've completed a task and you find yourself Facebook stalking to kill time while you wait for your next assignment, resist the urge! Work on something else or ask a colleague if she needs some help.

99. If you're on time, you're late. Always do your very best to arrive early to work, to meetings, or to a work function. Don't walk in at the time requested. Arrive early instead. Punctuality shows that you have respect for your coworkers, that you're excited about your work, and that you want to be there. Excuses like "I had to walk my puppy," "The line at Starbucks was out the door," or "My hair took longer to blow-dry than normal" are lame. If you have a real emergency or other issue, call and email your boss. Tell her when you'll arrive. Apologize!

100. Don't develop a mañana mentality. If something can be done today, don't leave it for tomorrow ... or the next day ... or next week.

101. How hard are you willing to work? Can you spell "promotion"? If you're passionate about your work and you want to stand out, you're going to have to make sacrifices. You may have to come in on a weekend or skip happy hour with the girls from time to time. When you find yourself frustrated and your panties are in a bunch because work is cutting into "you time," think big picture. Remind yourself that if you're not willing to make sacrifices, you're really not willing to be successful.

102. Employers like doers, not talkers, so get things done and stop whining. Be sure you back up your words with actions. A great way to gain respect from your coworkers early on is by always being true to your word, from the second you step into your job on the first day! Here's a general rule to follow: under-promise and over-deliver. By doing so, you'll always beat expectations.

103. Complacency will get you nowhere fast. Even if you think your boss adores you (and she may very well think you're great), you always have room for improvement. Go above and beyond the job description, and beat your employer's expectations of you. When you receive a compliment, a raise, or a bonus, use that as motivation to be even better.

104. Try this: Set objectives for yourself every morning by writing them down or entering a note into your phone. To-do lists are lukewarm commitments. Think of them as to-accomplish lists. You can even write down an inspirational quote at the top of your page that will motivate you throughout the day.

THE BOSS LADY SAYS

ARE YOU A GOAL-E GIRL?

My motto on Facebook (from an old postcard my mother sent me) is "A cowgirl gets up early in the morning, decides what she wants to do, and does it."

Set clear daily, weekly, monthly, and even yearly goals for yourself. Make lists. (If you write things down, they are more likely to get done!) Show your lists to your boss, discuss them, and make sure that you agree on tasks. Then, just get stuff done! Be ambitious, but not delusional. Excuses are for wimps and whiners.

Of course, things come up that can derail you. Computer glitches, meetings that throw off your schedule, and even weather can mess up a deadline. Stuff happens.

If you miss a deadline, analyze what went wrong and figure out a way to avoid it next time.

FIVE THINGS TO DO EVERY WEEK

1. Have a meeting with your boss to discuss projects and get feedback on your performance.* If you're clear on goals and getting constant input, you'll never be late or surprised.

2. Learn one new thing.

3. Do something fun, educational, or inspirational outside of work.

4. Put at least five dollars away for the future.

5. Set goals for the next week (personal and business).

*Make this happen! Even if your boss is scatterbrained or is "too busy to talk" sometimes, don't give up. We bosses love persistence and proactivity.

THINGS TO TALK ABOUT WITH YOUR BOSS
(EVEN WHEN YOU BELIEVE YOU HAVE NOTHING TO SAY)

☐ Tell her where you are with projects and assignments.

☐ If you don't have enough to do, ask for more.

☐ If you're confused, fess up and ask questions.

IF YOU ARE UNHAPPY ABOUT SOMETHING

☐ Do not whine or moan or get petulant.

☐ Stay positive and on message.

☐ Ask questions first ("Why aren't trainees invited to the weekly planning meeting?").

☐ Offer a useful suggestion with a benefit to the company or your boss ("If I could attend that meeting, I'd get my reports done faster and would understand more about the business").

☐ Respect a "no" or a "not now." Although championing things you believe in is a sign of leadership, your boss views herself as the voice of authority. You might ultimately be able to change her mind, but gather your facts first and approach your cause with composure, not anger or a sense of entitlement.

chapter eight

The Workplace Menagerie

Think of your colleagues as a (dysfunctional) animal family of sorts. Your coworkers come in a variety of shapes, sizes, moods, and species and some have many different spots, depending on the day of the week. Maintaining and building relationships with the many creatures at work can at times be even more challenging than the work itself!

You may not always agree with what they say and do, but you have to figure out a way to make it work and build productive, working relationships. Your colleagues may drive you nuts, skeeve you out, piss you off, and make you want to cry, but if you want your career to soar, you're going to have to learn how to suck it up and focus on the business at hand.

Follow our advice and peacefully coexist with any workplace species you encounter!

Be Beloved by Your Colleagues

Building positive, productive relationships with colleagues could mean the difference between work being a living hell and career heaven.

105. Be a lover, not a hater. When a colleague gets a promotion or nails a big project, compliment her sincerely. Secure women are able to praise their colleagues' good work and achievements. You could even send a note or flowers! Then, the next time you do something great, just watch: that person will be one of the first people to congratulate you!

106. Start a conga line of support (figuratively, of course) with your colleagues. Like people watching a real conga line, your coworkers will be reluctant to join at first, but once they see how much fun everyone else is having, they'll follow suit. Remember that respect, admiration, and good will are contagious. Watch as your colleagues all join your line and start being more supportive of one another.

107. Be a team player rather than a diva by stepping in and helping colleagues with an assignment when they need it. One day when you need a favor, they'll have your back. If you're working on a new project and think a colleague might be interested, ask her if she'd like to get involved. Supervisors often evaluate employees' performances based on their ability to collaborate and work well with others.

108. Own your mistakes and don't point fingers at your colleagues or boss. When you mess up—and it will happen—do whatever's necessary to rectify the situation, apologize for it quickly and sincerely, and move on. Let's say you made a doozy of an error at work and your boss gave you the mean face. Learn to dust yourself off and heal your bruises fast. Focus your energy on learning from what you did wrong and getting it right the next time. You're bound to slip and fall along the way to building your career. Just be sure you walk away from the situation learning something.

109. Look for patterns. If you repeatedly make the same types of errors, perhaps you need to ask more questions to clarify assignments or request additional out-of-work training. Ask yourself if the job is really the right fit for you. Better to bow out gracefully before you get booted out.

110. Be confident...not arrogant. Admit when you don't have the answers and be willing to learn from your colleagues and more experienced people at work. And they will appreciate your willingness to listen and learn.

111. Get to know the people you work with. Ask lots of questions and create opportunities to work with many different people. Understanding the history of your coworkers (at their current job and in past positions) will also give you insight into why they are the way they are.

112. Speak well of others at the water cooler. When your colleagues pick up on the fact that you always speak nicely of others rather than using any opportunity to bash a colleague behind her back, they'll recognize you as a genuine, no-nonsense, trustworthy coworker.

113. Align yourself with people who reflect your interests and values. If you spot someone who has a job you'd like to have someday, ask her about what she does and how she got there.

Boss Bonding

You may not like your boss. You may even loathe her at times, but if you want to survive in your position, get a raise, or score a great letter of recommendation down the line, you're going to have to make the best of the situation you're in and start bonding. Boss bonding is all about creating a healthy relationship between the two of you. Believe it or not, bonding with the head honcho is easier than you'd think!

114. No matter what you think of your boss, learn to respect and work with her. Part of adjusting to work is having to deal with people who get under your skin. Everyone has habits and quirks! Knowing what they are and striving to accommodate them is key.

115. Don't become your boss's lapdog. Office suck-ups are despised by their colleagues. When you receive attention or even accolades only because you're your boss's snitch, you betray your colleagues' trust and your integrity is put into question.

116. Be sure your boss knows she can trust you with confidential information, and always tell her the truth. Keep any conversations between the two of you. "Sharing" private conversations is a dirty habit that, in the long run, will damage your credibility.

117. Don't fake it. If your boss asks you to execute on a number of items in a meeting but you don't understand what she really needs, don't pretend you understand in an attempt to "not look dumb," only to go back back to your cube feeling completely lost. Your mediocre work will annoy your boss later on, and you'll likely wind up redoing the assignment—and wasting time! So before you head back to your cube, speak up! Make sure you understand your assignments. If you've jotted down a number of assignments and/or deliverables, ask your boss if you can repeat them back to her to ensure you've got everything down. Also, discuss priorities so you can rank-order the tasks.

118. Open the floor to questions and feedback. Good bosses welcome good questions from and conversations with their employees. Just be sure to approach your boss at an appropriate time, or even better, ask her if you can schedule a thirty-minute weekly meeting. Offer to come in early, stay late, or sacrifice a lunch to meet. Some alone time with the boss will do you a world of good and it will give you both a chance to get to know each other better.

119. Be promotable. Early on in your career, you're going to have to do tasks and assignments that you're not going to love and you might think to yourself, "I didn't go to college to make photocopies for my boss and arrange her travel!" But suck it up, because if you want something badly enough, you'll do whatever it takes to make it happen. If you are constantly cranky and bitter, no one will want to promote you or work with you elsewhere.

120. Keep it real with the boss lady. The time will come when you'll be unhappy at work, perhaps even with your boss because of something she did or said. Schedule a meeting with your boss and make her aware of the matter's urgency. When you sit down to talk, speak your mind in a professional way without attacking or offending.

121. Do not gossip with your colleagues about your frustrations with your boss. Give her the respect and courtesy of sharing your feelings with her to her face. If she catches wind of your displeasure through the grapevine, it might really tick her off and close her off to wanting to understand what was at the root of the problem.

GET IN YOUR BOSS'S FACE (NOT UP HER BUTT)

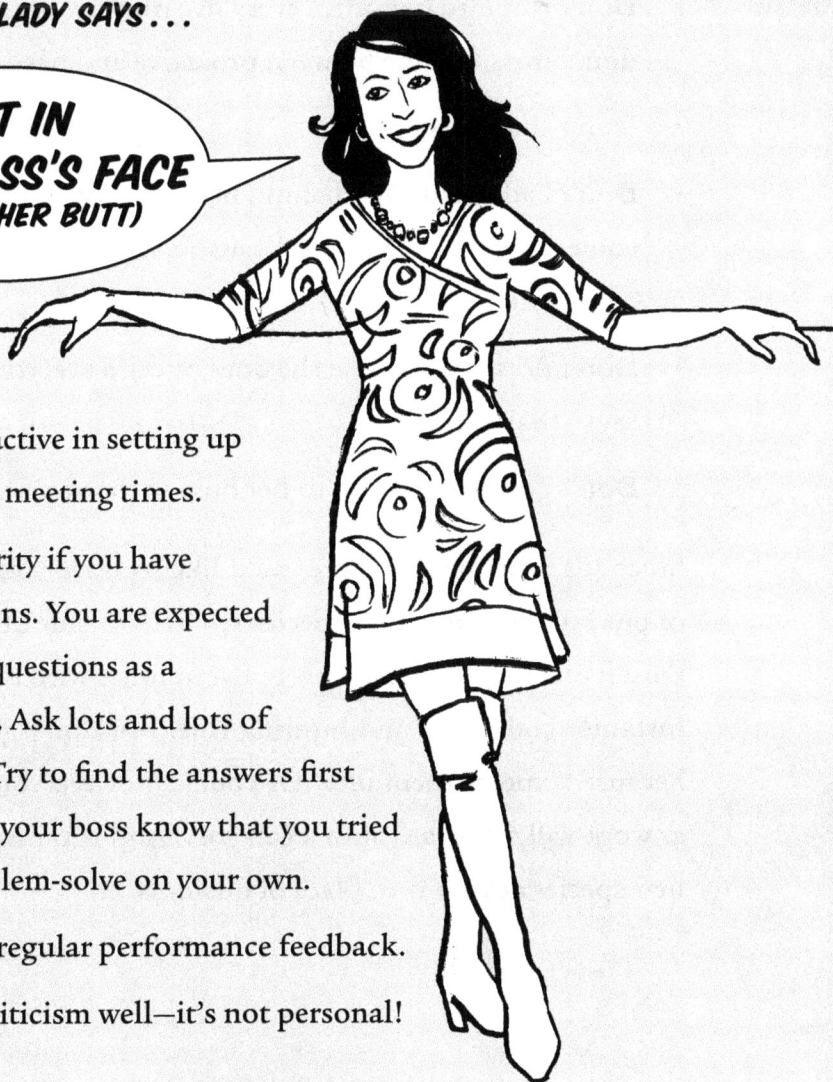

- Be proactive in setting up regular meeting times.
- Get clarity if you have questions. You are expected to ask questions as a newbie. Ask lots and lots of them. Try to find the answers first and let your boss know that you tried to problem-solve on your own.
- Solicit regular performance feedback.
- Take criticism well—it's not personal!

- Do extra meaningful things to stand out (e.g., work late on a key project, offer to get coffee when you're going out for a cup for yourself, share relevant articles related to your industry).

- Ask how you can get ahead.

- Don't run into her office every five minutes with questions; don't cross the line between proactive and needy.

- Don't share gossip.

- Don't bad-mouth her behind her back. Even if she does something truly heinous, discuss it with her directly in confidence.

- Don't dress exactly like she does or echo everything she says—that's creepy!

- Don't go over her head to her boss without permission.

Since it's a jungle out there, we'd like to leave you with a few of our favorite workplace species spotted outside of their cages. Observe, enjoy, and learn how to live at peace with them. Do not instantly grab a net and hunting rifle. But don't get too close because some of them bite! Of course, not everyone you meet at work will fall neatly into a category. And you may encounter new species at your own place of business.

Creature	Characteristics	How to Deal
Party Pammy	The wild child—loves hooking up and happy hours. Work? Not so much.	Set boundaries with her. Don't care if she thinks you're a party pooper.
Rumor Ruth	Snoopy and relishes gossip. Information = power. And some of her information is just not true.	Don't be sucked into her shenanigans. She'll turn on you in a heartbeat and *you'll* be rumor-fodder. Act disinterested and get back to work.
Me-Me-Me Mimi	The narcissist. It's always about her. Who else is there to talk about?	Smile, nod, and get back to work. Hard to change this creature.
In Crisis Crissy	So much drama, you'd think she was on Bravo. Work…life…there's always something major happening.	Stay calm and act the voice of reason, especially when you're on work teams together. Make a plan and speak softly.
Shrinking Violet	Oh so timid. Even she forgets she's in the room.	Lead by example. She'll see you exuding confidence and assertiveness. Include her in conversation and ask for her opinions.
Debbie Downer	Parched because her glass is always half empty.	Don't let her negativity bum you out. Keep upbeat and focused on the task at hand.

Creature	Characteristics	How to Deal
Spacey Gracie	The lost soul who never knows what she wants.	If you can take her under her wing and help her succeed, that's wonderful. But if you find yourself unfocused after talking to her, steer clear.
Creeping Tom	Enjoys lurking, creeping, soulful stares, and long walks on the beach.	Don't entertain his behavior. If he makes you feel uncomfortable, tell him so before you resort to a restraining order!
Bitchy Boss Betty	Makes unreasonable demands and humiliates people in public.	Schedule a private one-on-one meeting to discuss how her "style" is affecting your work performance and attitude.
Two-Faced Tammy	Sometimes acts like your best friend and then turns on you suddenly.	Keep your distance and learn to read her moods. Do not totally trust her "up" times.
Subtle Sue	A cruel one on the sly.	Call her out in the moment. Direct a question at her if she's ignoring your presence.
Fabulous Franny	You!	Enough said. Read this book carefully and keep being fabulous.

Have you encountered new creatures in your work zoo? If so, we'd love to hear about them. Come visit our website and help us build the work animal kingdom (queendom!).

chapter nine

Play Nice!

How you choose to handle your coworkers' (as well as your own) attitudes and emotions at work can keep a minor incident from escalating into a nuclear disaster. You can do your very best to forge strong relationships at work, but conflict is inevitable!

You may find yourself taking home resentment and frustration rather than actual work assignments. You spend enough time with your colleagues as it is; we'll help you learn how not to invite them home with you—especially not to bed! No one wants to spend a night tossing and turning because of a conflict at work. And because mean girls abound, we're going to teach you how to deal with women whose intentions are cruel and catty. You'll approach your work and your colleagues more positively, and your newly centered energy at work will manifest better outcomes for yourself.

You'll never be able to control how someone else behaves, but what you do have control over is how you react, what you say and do, and how you approach a tough situation. Girls who play nice will always win at the end of the day. Just don't be a doormat—there's a big difference!

Work Wars

When you work with the same people day in and day out, conflict is unavoidable. But when handled the right way, any argument—whether it's a small ground skirmish or a nuclear meltdown—can be defused when addressed constructively. The battle scars will eventually fade and you might even get closer to the warring faction as a result of the resolution process.

It's important to keep in mind that when conflict arises, it's usually not personal. Business is business, and when one of your colleagues seems to be at odds with you, ask yourself: "Is this person really attacking *me*?" More often than not, it's not about you.

When your panties are in a bunch and your temperature is rising and you're tempted to fire off a sassy email, the pointers detailed here will help resolve conflict.

Let's say that a coworker just accused you of something you didn't do. Or your boss chewed you out after you handed in a project.

122. Use your head...not your heart. Stay calm, professional, and balanced. Sticking it to someone might alleviate anger at the moment, but you'll wind up deeply regretting the decision, perhaps just a few minutes later. You may say things you'll regret. And you won't have taken enough time to analyze the situation and gather facts.

123. Take a deep breath. In fact, take a breather and step away from the situation. If you're face to face with someone, say, "I think it's best if we address this a little later, when we've both calmed down." Then walk away. Take a ten-minute break and pull yourself together at a nearby café or in the ladies' room.

124. Resolve conflicts in person, even if an email was the instigator. The written word is powerful and emails are like diamonds: they last forever. Don't attempt to rectify a situation with an email. Ask to meet with the person instead.

125. Get your facts straight while you're cooling off. While you're recalibrating your thoughts and sipping on a latte, consider whether you've missed something. Be empathetic: put yourself in the other person's shoes for a minute. Why was your boss short with you? Perhaps she is under pressure from *her* boss and your lateness or errors on a project put her in a tough position. Maybe a coworker is jealous because you are getting all the plum assignments and she is feeling threatened.

126. Resolve the conflict soon. When you've both calmed down, ask to meet with the "opposing party" in private as soon as possible. Conflict that's left to brew over time—even if it seems to go away—escalates because resentment builds in both parties.

127. Talk it out and put it to bed. Approach the person with whom you had the tiff calmly and matter-of-factly, and get over the urge to win. Listen to (and really hear) her point of view. Ask questions. When you set out to try to "win" an argument, your coworker's guard goes up and defense mode ensues. When you speak, share your perspective calmly. If your coworker feels that you're trying to see things through her eyes, she may eventually show you the same respect and you'll both come to an agreement.

128. Always remember that you're a professional—not a reality TV star—so never engage with someone if they attack you. If a coworker raises her voice or slams a door or a notebook, back down and continue to carry yourself civilly. Never retaliate by raising your voice or shouting back. No one ever wins a fight at work.

129. Move on...don't hold grudges.

In a Funk at Work?

We all have good days and some not-so-great ones, but you can't bring your home/friend/boyfriend issues into work with you. Here's what to do when your personal stuff is weighing on your work stuff.

130. Apply the law of attraction to work. You needn't be a tea-sipping yogi to make this work for you, at work! It's really quite simple. When you approach a work situation with negative thoughts and intentions because your personal life is stressing you, more often than not the outcome will be negative. You'll continue to attract negative circumstances and outcomes all day long. Your printer will stop working, your colleague will say something you don't like, you'll get into an argument with a coworker. A positive mind-set, on the other hand, can help you achieve your goals and attract better circumstances to you.

131. Hit the mental reset button. When negative, disempowering thoughts arise, you have the power to delete them with an empowering thought. When your boss criticizes you, rather than thinking about all the things you could have done or why you're not good enough, press Delete and think about all of the things you do well and what you can do (using her advice) to be better.

When you're down in the dumps at work, rather than lashing out at a colleague, try these simple funk-busters:

- Read an uplifting quote or two.

- Listen to a positive playlist that makes you feel good.

- Take a fiver (a five-minute break).

- Think about a recent accomplishment. Remember the good feelings that you had in the moment.

- Stop dwelling on what's wrong about a person or situation. Instead, ask yourself, "What can I learn from this situation?"

- Make plans for that evening or weekend. Get your head outside of work for a few minutes.

The Mean Girl Epidemic

Women sometimes backstab other women in the workplace like it's part of the job description. It should be a white-collar crime! A variety of factors like insecurity, jealousy, peer pressure, and competition influence women to harm other women. Rather than talk out any issues, women attempt to act "lady-like" with cruel tactics like gossiping and snubbing, or more subtle torture techniques like ignoring a female colleague's presence.

Sadly, some of these behaviors start in the playground and carry through to the conference room, especially as many women feel as if they are competing with other women for promotions, the attention of their bosses, or even relationships with influential peers. You may be approached with juicy gossip and be expected to join in bitch-slapping others—misery loves company, after all! You could even become the target. But behaving like a gossip or witch will only make you appear more like a crazed reality TV star than a polished professional, so watch and learn from the true ladies (and the gentlemen!) at work and resist the urge to become a gossip girl or a pit bull.

132. Do not allow yourself to get caught up in any gossiping or backstabbing. If a coworker approaches you with "inside information," let her know that you don't want to be on the rumor circuit. Saying something as simple as "I really don't know anything about that" as opposed to "Oh, really? What else did you hear?" makes it clear that you don't want to be a major player in dirt-spreading.

133. If, on the other hand, you find out that *you* are the target of rumors, handle the situation based on its effect on your career. If someone is spreading information about you that could have an impact on your future, then you are fully justified in letting the "spreader" know that you are aware of the gossip and that you want to set the record straight and prevent the rumor from continuing. Sometimes, just letting a gossip know that you're wise to her will compel her to choose a different target next time (or even to rethink her behavior).

How to Kill a Mean Girl with Kindness

134. Calmly approach your attacker. Ask her if she has time to talk privately or schedule a meeting. Then say, "I understand that you're unhappy with me. Can we talk about it?"

135. Never throw anyone under the bus by revealing your sources to the mean girl. She may try to redirect her focus to the person who ratted her out, but don't let her take control. Bring the conversation back to the issue between the two of you.

136. Keep your conversation about productivity, performance, and profit—not emotions. Tell her that your work is suffering because of her actions. Tell her that you want to work on your relationship and ask her for her opinion. And listen to her, even if the sound of her voice irks you!

137. Come to a conclusion about how the two of you can work better together. Be firm with her. Say that you'd appreciate her coming to you in the future if she has any issues with you.

Here's how to beat a passive aggressor at her own game, no matter what the "if" (many of these tips were adapted from *Bitch Slap: When Women Misbehave at Work,* by Nancy A. Shenker—aka The Boss Lady—available on Amazon.com or at www.nunumedia.com and www.buoypoint.com).

138. If a coworker sends you an obviously nasty but indirect email, email her back, simply saying: "Are you upset with me? If so, I'd be glad to talk about the situation in person."

139. If a woman ignores your presence in a group by either not including you in the discussion, not making eye contact with you, or acting like she doesn't see you, speak louder or repeat yourself. She may be trying to intimidate you and cut you out of the group, so don't simply sit there in silence.

140. If the mean girl makes a snide remark in a group of people, call her out in the moment by calmly and assertively saying, "May I ask what you meant by that?" You're pleasantly telling her in a group setting that you won't take her abuse.

141. If a colleague suddenly unfriends you on Facebook, just let it be. You have lots of real and virtual friends; you don't need her to validate you.

142. If a coworker makes a face, or rolls her eyes, or emits a witch-like cackle, ask her, "Is everything OK?" When the face-maker replies with a "Why do you ask?" you can explain, "You made a strange face/noise in the meeting."

143. If your colleague's gossiping and cruel behavior persists, don't hesitate to speak to your boss about the situation. You should never feel uncomfortable in your working environment or be anxious about going to work. But choose your words carefully. Let your boss know that you've tried to rectify the situation on your own, and ask for suggestions on how to improve the working relationship. You don't want to sound as if you're ratting out a coworker or you're incapable of dealing with your own problems.

GOOD GIRLS CAN BE POWER PLAYERS

Having worked throughout my career with women as bosses, coworkers, and employees, I have found that some women tend to bring their emotional baggage (and, in some cases, an entire set of mismatched luggage) into the workplace and can turn conflict into schoolyard squabbles. I have never heard a male coworker making a comment about another guy's necktie pattern or whispering about "the new guy" in the lunchroom.

My daughters grew up playing team sports and, as a result, have become team players in school and life as well. My generation was less about teams and more about individual achievement and competition, and I have experienced lots of bad behavior among women in the workplace as a result.

As a boss, I tend to think less of women who can't get along with each other at work—who consistently spread rumors or disparage successful women...who don't help other women who are struggling in their jobs...who focus on personal appearance over work performance . . . who are overly flirty with male managers in order to get ahead rather than focusing on the quality of their work.

We women are still learning how to hold on to our feminine side while being taken seriously in the working world. Great women leaders are strong *and* kind. Remember that! And we can all be bitchy from time to time. But there's a difference between acting bitchy and being a real bitch! It all has to do with intent to hurt.

chapter ten

Off the Clock
What's Going On After Work?

After 6 p.m. (or whenever you're off the clock) is
"you time," and it has to be time well spent.
Your out-of-office behavior should support your
career goals and dreams, and it shouldn't be
self-destructive. We want to help you develop great
habits now, so your lifestyle supports your career
goals and chances of success. Your energy level,
moods, and self-esteem all have an impact
on your work performance.

But lots of temptations and distractions can derail any smart girl with a good head on her shoulders and a college degree. Happy hour is so enticing, especially when you're single and ready to mingle with some cuties at the bar, and who doesn't love a company party where everyone can cut loose and get wild? So you think...But when you're living in the moment without thinking about your future, mistakes become compounded. One weekend of partying hard, the wrong hook-up, or major girlfriend drama can lead to an unproductive workweek. An impromptu shopping spree can lead to more mindless shopping. Before you know it, your closet is filled but your bank account is overdrawn. When you lack focus off the clock, your career and your health ultimately suffer.

Redefine Playtime

144. Don't parlay that same sort of partying you got away with in college into your new postgrad life. Don't deprive yourself of good times, but you need to know when to call it quits so your future isn't sacrificed.

145. Treat happy hour as a treat, not a daily indulgence. When you go out for drinks frequently after work, the boozing can make getting up early difficult and lead to bad decision after bad decision. Drinking too much will take you away from reality, and you'll lose sight of what it is you truly want in life.

146. If you must have a cocktail when you're with colleagues (especially during the workweek), limit yourself to one drink. Then, call it quits, even if your coworkers give you a hard time. This will save you from any embarrassing "next days" at work.

147. Watch the weekend partying. Don't save up an entire work week of "laying low" only to spend the weekend intoxicated for forty-eight hours. That time can be better used to try out a new athletic activity, read the Sunday paper, visit a museum, download a new book, take a class, explore the city, take a weekend trip, or revamp that résumé.

THE BOSS LADY SAYS ₒ ◯ ◯

WEREN'T YOU WEARING THAT YESTERDAY?

Your boss may not see you at 2 a.m. in the club, but she can sure see the hangover at the 8 a.m. meeting. Your personal life is personal, but the impact on your work performance can affect your chance of a promotion. Believe me. I know. I once fell asleep proofreading at my desk after a 4 a.m. "walk of shame" back to my apartment and a whopping three hours of sleep. Thankfully, my boss didn't notice, and my partying days in the late 1970s went the way of discos and polyester. But we bosses can be very observant. You may think you've pulled it together and have reported to work as your best self…but telltale signs like repeated trips to the coffee maker, dark eye circles, and sloppy work errors are a tip-off to your boss that your life after work is more important than what goes on from nine to five. And if you want a shot at a promotion more than you want a jello shot, you'll keep your life pretty clean from Sunday night through Thursday night.

Who Are You Hanging Out With?

148. Surround yourself with A-listers and gently cut back time spent with naysayers, slackers, and drifters. This may sound harsh, but the company you keep should be people who motivate and inspire you. And expand your circle to include role models. It's easy to hate on others who seem to have it all together, but perhaps you can learn from them.

149. As you evolve into the "better you," don't go missing on anyone because that's the coward's way out. Just tell the detractor/distractor that you're "really focused on your career right now" when she asks you to do something that doesn't further your goal. You never know. Your good habits might rub off on a slacker friend and inspire her!

Discover Endorphins and Eat Clean

Even if you're a couch potato who loves potatoes and have been cruising along at your ninth-grade weight for years, the time of entering the work world (which can be sedentary) is also a good time to become active in your personal life.

150. Get yourself moving. Whether you love it or hate it, exercise is a must. Working out will get your energy level up in the morning and help you decompress after a long day of work. Instead of unwinding at happy hour, have a healthier happy hour at the gym; try a class like kickboxing, spin, yoga, or Pilates. Gyms and parks can be a great place to network (and meet guys too)!

151. If you don't have a gym membership, go for a walk or a run after work. Get your friends together to do workouts online or on DVDs to get your fitness on in the comfort of your home. You don't have to have an expensive gym membership to stay active, so don't use that as an excuse.

152. You are what you eat and drink. What are you fueling your mind and body with on a daily basis? Keep processed foods out of your body and eat more foods that come from the earth, not a factory! Buy a reusable water bottle, and fill it throughout the day to stay hydrated.

153. Be kind to yourself and your body. A lettuce leaf, a Red Bull, and a handful of laxatives do not constitute a good day of nutrition, even if you indulged in a pint of Ben & Jerry's the night before! Fad diets and yo-yo dieting can really do a number on your body and mind over time. Make moderation your mantra.

154. Cooking after work is a fun way to eat well too. It's very gratifying to prepare your own meals, and you'll know exactly where your food came from! You and your girlfriends can take turns hosting simple dinner parties; the get-togethers don't have to be extravagant, and cooking could develop into a fun and healthy new passion.

Feed Your Head Well Too!

155. What are you reading before and after work? Aside from any material you need to read for work, you should read regularly to keep your mind active and engaged. When you're well read, you can contribute to all sorts of interesting conversations, and you can use your knowledge to your advantage.

156. Aim to read at least two articles—either news-related or from a magazine—or at least one chapter from your favorite chick lit, mystery, business book, or classic novel every day. Gossip magazines don't count—unless you're building a career as a Hollywood publicist!

157. If you have a commute into work and then home, use that time to its fullest. Listen to an audio book. Use business travel time to catch up on reading too. (And, of course, you can bring your reading material with you to the gym.)

Zzzzzzzz . . .

158. Get your beauty sleep; eight hours is ideal. You'll function better at work, have more energy, and be able to get through a day's work without having to chug cups of coffee or cans of energy drinks. Your body will love you for it, and you'll soon get used to hitting the sheets early. You'll wake up feeling energized and full of life the next morning!

159. Disconnect from your cell when it's bedtime and use a real alarm clock. You're on your phone all day long so the two of you could use some healthy separation when it's time to hit the sheets. Power down at night.

160. Start a dream journal (online or in a notebook). Your dreams can tell you a lot about what's in your subconscious. Compare notes with girlfriends and maybe even post your dreams on GoogleDocs to share and analyze. Sometimes what's in your head at night can be as entertaining as what goes on during the day!

You Got the Urge to Splurge?

You're working to make money, right? Now is a great time to get smarter about managing income and outflows. Debt is as ugly as wrinkles and cellulite. When paychecks finally start rolling into your bank account, you may feel euphoric. After years of asking your parents for dough and slaving at unpaid internships, you want to spend money like it's no one's biz once you're finally making it—manicures and pedicures each week, expensive lunches, a new pair of shoes on a whim, a pricey martini or two. Who cares?! Your gut may tell you that you probably shouldn't be spending wantonly, and you should learn to listen to that naggy little voice.

161. Make a budget. If you're not a "math girl," enlist a friend to help you. Many local schools also teach classes in money management for women.

162. Calculate what you have coming in monthly, less any fixed expenses (loans, rent, food, bills, etc.). Then decide how much you'd like to save per month and figure out how much you then actually have left to play with. If you're like most young pros, your starting salary isn't anything to write home about, so you'll have to be a savvy consumer.

163. Before making a purchase, ask yourself: Is this something I *really* need? If you can't decide right way, sleep on it. If you're still jonesing for it the next day, go back and purchase it. But unless Mom and Dad are funding your existence, know when to put it down and walk away.

164. If you don't have it, don't spend it. Credit cards can be evil, so beware. You might consider canceling and shredding your credit cards, or maybe holding onto just one for emergencies.

Cut Corners and Save!

165. Make friends with Groupon and local bargain sites. Look for special offers on Foursquare. Search for travel specials when you go on vacation. Enter contests for free stuff (but make sure you aren't getting on a million email lists and making yourself a spam target). You can even download grocery coupons and look through newspapers for sales. But don't buy stuff you don't need just because it's a bargain.

166. Start bringing your lunch to work a few days per week. If you do go out to lunch at a casual spot, save money on a soft drink and bring your reusable water bottle in your purse.

167. Skip that morning latte. Make coffee at home and bring it to work in a reusable coffee mug. There's four dollars or more right back in your pocket!

168. Walk or use mass transportation. If you live in an urban area, stop spending your money on cabs. They're expensive and they're dirty polluters! Imagine how sexy and toned your legs will get if you walk around more!

169. Work on the wardrobe. Buy versatile pieces that you can mix and match. Limit yourself to one or two trendy items per season. Those wide-legged pants or over-the-knee boots will wind up in the back of the closet next fall, so if you *must* have them, don't spend a lot on them.

170. Give yourself a mani and pedi. It might not feel as luxurious, but you'll save a boatload of cash by doing your nails yourself!

171. You can sometimes save money on your hair care by allowing yourself to serve as a "practice model" for students. Risky, but frugal!

Yes . . . There IS a Test

Each week—when you're vegging out on Sunday evening is a good time—reflect on your previous week and take this quiz. Answer it honestly; it's meant to keep you on track so you can see what areas of your life outside of work need some attention. Study your answers when you're through. Don't beat yourself up if you had a bad week. Use the quiz as motivation to do better next week!

- I exercised _____ times this week.
- I read at least two news articles or one e-zine or at least one chapter of a book _____ out of seven days. (Remember, tabloids don't count!)
- I slept an average of _____ hours per night.
- I went out for happy hour and/or drinks with friends _____ times this week.

- When I went out for cocktails, I had approximately _____ drinks per happy hour/night out.
- I watched _____ hours of TV and movies.
- I spent approximately _____ on meals out.
- I splurged on _____ this past week.
- I ate well _____ out of seven days. (Be honest!)

THE BOSS LADY SAYS ○ ○ ○ **OVERTIME, SCHMOVERTIME!**

And it may seem obvious, but if your boss asks you to work late or on a weekend, you should say "Of course!" Even if you have regular work hours, the willingness to put in extra time shows your boss that you take your career seriously. Unless you have a nonrefundable plane ticket or an invitation to attend a family reunion, plans can usually be changed. (It's OK, too, to let your boss know that you made the sacrifice too. You'll score extra points.) Beware, however, of bosses who expect you to work nights and weekends constantly without any compensation. A fine line exists between diligence and exploitation. If you feel your management is taking advantage of you, speak up (but don't whine, please!).

PART THREE

Quitting Time?

You'll eventually want to hit the road and leave a job, so our next section will advise you on how to say buh-bye to your boss in the most graceful way, leaving your colleagues and supervisors wishing you well and toasting to your future.

But before you go anywhere, be absolutely sure you're leaving for the right reasons. If you truly hate coming to work four out of five days a week, it may be time to go. Be sure, however, that you've thoroughly explored all the options (like a new position in a different department, an exciting new assignment, or a transfer to another location).

If you do decide to move on, we'll show you how to exit well and ensure that even if that next position doesn't work out the way you planned, you stay professional and employable.

chapter eleven

Promotion Motion or Inertia?

You may want to leave a job because you feel like you've
"hit a wall." No one ever got promoted because she
demanded it. If you're generally happy at your job, but just
want more responsibility or more money, first follow
The Boss Lady's tips for moving up the ladder.

172. Ask your boss exactly what you need to demonstrate in order to step up that next rung. Shadow someone who is actually doing that job and ask lots of questions.

173. Show that you can really do the job you want next. Take classes, volunteer, ask for special assignments, and continually ask for (and accept) feedback.

174. When you do ask for a raise or promotion, build a fact-based case. No one ever gets a raise or a promotion simply because she needs it. (If that were the case we'd all be millionaires!) Give specific examples of results you have achieved in your job, money you've saved the company, new clients you've brought in, or important projects you completed. You can even create a PowerPoint or report and give it to your boss as a written reminder of all that you've done.

175. Do not threaten to leave or throw a tantrum.

176. Be patient. Ask your boss for a specific time frame for decision-making.

177. Timing is important. Do not ask for a raise when your boss is rushing out the door for a meeting or immediately after your company announces major layoffs.

But maybe it's really not about moving up within your company. Perhaps you're simply burned-out, bored, or looking for new places, people, and challenges. All good things, and maybe not-so-good things, must come to an end. You may need to change jobs a couple of times before you figure out exactly what turns you on. It's like dating; you give several prospects a shot before you find the one. You'll eventually get to a point when you'll be ready to move on to greener pastures. You may decide the industry you're in just isn't your calling, you might just not be clicking with the people you work with and for, or you may have simply been offered an exciting opportunity.

Is It Time to Say Buh-Bye?

If one or several of these points pertain to you, consider updating that résumé and cruising job sites.

- You truly don't enjoy the work you do on a daily basis and no one else's job at the company seems any better than yours.

- You wake up dreading work, and you find yourself depressed on Sunday nights.

- You don't feel challenged by the work. Even after you've talked it over with your boss, nothing has changed. The work bores you, plain and simple.

- Your employer will not give you a raise (or a timetable for giving you one) even though you have gotten great evaluations and are doing everything she asks.

- You're getting mediocre (or simply bad) performance reviews and cannot seem to turn things around. It's better to leave before you get fired.

- You've hooked up with several dudes in the surrounding cubes (or have made other really bad choices) and now you can't seem to stop the whispering throughout the company.

- The work goes against your belief system. You feel uncomfortable every day because your job, for one reason or another, doesn't reflect your values.

- You've gossiped so much about all your colleagues that you're left with no allies.

Here are some general words of wisdom that will benefit your career over time.

178. Stay at least a year at a job, unless it is so unbearable that you cry yourself to sleep every night and you've talked repeatedly to your boss about your concerns. Employers look for people who give jobs a chance before they bail.

179. Take pride in the job at hand. Even if you don't see yourself working in your current role for long, be someone who carries out each task with pride, not with anger, resentment, or a sense of entitlement. And when the day arrives when you finally decide to move on, your boss will be delighted to send you off with a letter of recommendation.

180. Be realistic. Work is work. Before you launch an aggressive job search, sit down and talk to your boss about what you like (and don't like) about your job. Take responsibility for your own career advancement.

THE BOSS LADY SAYS

DON'T BE A RAT

You should always talk to your immediate supervisor first before you speak with her supervisors, other senior-level people, or human resources. If you have a suggestion about how your job could be made more rewarding, go to your boss with a detailed proposal. We boss ladies like solutions...not random complaining.

If you ever have to directly confront a "bully boss," begin the conversation with "I would really like to improve our working relationship so that I can be more productive and effective." Focus on the behavior ("When you do..., my reaction is...") rather than personalizing your comments ("You bully me"). You just may end up shaking hands and agreeing to some new ground rules.

chapter twelve

Buh-Bye

Once you've carefully determined that it's time
to get your search on (or if you've been offered
a new job that you simply can't refuse),
here's how to keep your wits about you and
resign beautifully before you bounce.

Your Search Party

181. When you're ready to throw yourself back into the market, be sure that you keep up your work ethic at your job so your employer doesn't get suspicious.

182. Don't, under any circumstance, job-hunt or take hunt-related calls on your company's computer or phone system, even if you think that no one will ever know. Imagine what would happen if you walked away from your computer and accidentally left a search site open on your monitor. At the very least, it could be uncomfortable for you.

183. Your current employer should never find out that you're interviewing or corresponding with a job prospect on company time. If your company's dress code is business casual and you walk in wearing a suit, people may figure out what's going on! Instead, take a personal day or unpaid time off.

Bow Out Gracefully

A resignation conversation can be as anxiety-provoking as that first job interview, so plan it well and handle it professionally.

184. Ask your boss for an in-person meeting as soon as you've accepted an offer. Give her no less than two weeks' notice, as anything short of this is unfair and unprofessional. She'll want to start her own candidate search to fill your position as soon as she can.

185. Ask specifically what needs to be transitioned and work out a plan for handing off work.

186. Although you can offer helpful suggestions for improving your job or company policy, under no circumstances should you trash the company or whine in an exit conversation. It only makes you look immature. Business people want business suggestions—not emotional outpourings or random complaints.

187. Don't make the mistake of telling your colleagues before you tell your boss. You may be gleeful and giddy, but refrain because it will get back to your boss before you've had the opportunity to respectfully tell her yourself. When you meet, discuss how your boss would like to inform your coworkers, but ultimately leave to her the decision as to how she wants to inform others.

188. Bring your A Game up to the very end, because you still have work that needs to get done! Continue with your responsibilities.

189. Arrive on time to work and meetings, and keep reminding yourself that you don't have to stick it out for too much longer! If you want to walk out with referrals and letters of recommendation, don't slack off in your final weeks.

190. Ask for recommendations and references from your colleagues and bosses. If you've been a superstar employee from the get-go, they'll all want to sing your praises.

191. Make sure your former colleagues have your new email address and telephone number, and be sure you have their personal email addresses so you can stay in touch.

THE BOSS LADY SAYS

> PLEASE, PLEASE, PLEASE STAY . . . I'LL DO ANYTHING!

Sometimes an employee will resign and a boss will do anything within reason to change her mind. I've been on both sides of the desk during these conversations. Accepting a counteroffer is usually a bad idea. If you've already accepted another offer, it's usually a *really* bad idea. The hiring company and your current employer may both view you as untrustworthy.

Saying goodbye to a stellar employee is gut-wrenching, and a good boss will always try to find out what she can do to change the outcome.

192. Behave at your going-away party and don't gloat. "I hope you're next!" is the kind of statement that can be demoralizing to those you're leaving behind. Exit on a high note.

193. Even after you're gone, watch what you say about your previous employer online. Do not bash your former company. You never know when you'll need a reference. Gossip is never a good idea... even when you've moved on.

If you generally like what you're doing but just have specific unmet career goals, give your boss a chance to keep you before you start a job hunt. Tell your boss honestly that you have been contemplating your next career move. Make a list of things you'd like to do more of or less of at your current company. And talk honestly about your expectations (including financial).

Although that conversation can be uncomfortable and scary, getting new opportunities at a place you know and like can be preferable to starting fresh in an unknown environment.

And, if you do end up leaving, at least you'll know you gave your boss a chance to hold on to you.

chapter thirteen

Stay Smart, Stay in Touch, Stay Employed

The time to push yourself and grow in your career is when you've got a great job and you're killing it. Smart girls don't simply go to work and come home, only to wake up and do it all again the next day. They stay on top of their game, learn from other successful professionals, and embrace challenges and the chance to meet new people.

Here's how to get ahead and get connected to the right people:

194. Join your alumni association. You don't have to contribute money to stay connected with your fellow grads. Get involved with your alma mater by checking out its website and reaching out to someone who handles alumni affairs. Ask your friends from college who are active with your school how they think you should get involved.

195. Join a professional women's group. Women's groups of all types abound, and they can be a wonderful way to meet women of all ages and backgrounds, so be supportive, and be supported.

196. Subscribe to three or more e-zines. Get great content sent to your inbox. You can read them when you have some spare time, either when you're walking to work, on the train, or at lunch.

197. Attend a conference. Be inspired by people who are experts in the field you're interested in. You'll get inside secrets from leading figures, and you'll digest an insane amount of practical knowledge to apply to your career. Some employers will even pay for you to attend a conference that's relevant to your job, so don't be afraid to ask if you can attend and explain why it will help you!

198. Practice networking even when you're not job-hunting. Continue to make connections with new, interesting people. You never know when just one contact might come in handy.

Even if you're as happy as can be in your position, get out there and keep meeting helpful professionals.

199. Have monthly lunches or calls with your mentor. Stay close with her and set up a time every month to talk. If you discover an interesting networking event or conference that you think she'd be interested in, ask her if she'd like to attend with you.

200. Talk to strangers. Whether you're at the gym, a café, shopping, or walking your dog, be interested in other people and strike up conversation with strangers. You'll find that your boldness will begin to work for you and your career!

201. Take a class (or two) at nights or on weekends. Some companies will even pay! Learn a second language, master a new computer program, or better your speaking, writing, and presenting skills.

202. Read, read, read. You can never be smart enough, so subscribe to your favorite news and magazine sites or download their apps. If you're a voracious reader, book clubs are another way to meet people!

203. Develop a specialty. Become really good at something that relates to your career or that might prove useful at work or in life—blogging, cooking, activism, social media, sports, environmentalism, fitness, knitting, making your own beauty products. The options are endless!

204. Use your LinkedIn network. Scan LinkedIn often to see what your connections are up to. Keep in touch with others and ask a few colleagues if they'd "recommend you."

205. Set specific goals and share them with an "accountability buddy." When you're slacking off, your buddy can call you out.

Your work doesn't end after you've read this chapter and neither does ours! We'll part ways, for now, with twelve ways to stay smart and connected at all times. We encourage you to stay connected with us, as well! We'd like to hear how you've applied this book to yor life and how it's helped you find your way. Send us an email, become our fan on Facebook, tweet us a shot of you reading this book, and comment on our website! If you're an old soul, we love written letters, too! Either way, we look forward to keeping in touch.

THE BOSS LADY SAYS

GOOD-BYE, GOOD LUCK, GOOD FORTUNE!

I graduated from college in 1977 and have had lots of jobs ... and lots of bosses ... since then.

I've messed up, hooked up, fessed up, and been bumped up. I've been hired, fired, humiliated, celebrated, and exasperated. I've hired, fired, and inspired others. I've been called lots of names (usually behind my back) and given all types of performance reviews. I've never cried at work (although I've come close). It's been a long and winding road, for sure.

And so, my advice for all you young women reading this book (whether it's on paper or on a screen) is remember that it's all a journey. It'll have great days and really sucky ones. And you'll make a lot of mistakes and you need to learn to own up to them and sometimes even laugh about them afterward. You should learn to analyze, know your facts, and ask for what you want.

1. You should speak and write clearly and well— and proofread!

2. You should use the telephone and not just texts and emails.

3. You should not take things personally.

4. You should take care of yourself and stay healthy.

5. You should stay smart by reading, watching, and listening.

6. You should be honest and fair—with yourself and others.

7. You should learn from those people who know things that you may not (yet).

8. You should be helpful and kind.

9. You should stay connected to other people and new ideas.

10. You should follow your passions. They may change over time. That's OK.

11. You should recommend this book to your friends and chat with us on our blog.

12. And you probably shouldn't hook up with the dude in the next cube.

Thank you!

About the Authors

Nancy A. Shenker

Nancy A. Shenker (aka The Boss Lady) has more than thirty years of experience as a marketer, writer, speaker, and innovator. Her publishing venture, nunu media™, is her most recent endeavor.

She considers herself a dual citizen of the traditional marketing world and the social media planet, and in both her corporate career and at theONswitch®, a boutique marketing consulting company she founded in 2003, she has helped a wide range of businesses—both small and large—launch, rebrand, and flourish.

She has held senior marketing positions at major brand companies—Citibank, MasterCard International, and Reed Exhibitions. Her consulting experience spans a wide range of industries, including retail, food, kids and education, fashion, sports, health and wellness, real estate and shelter, marketing services, technology, service businesses, and the event industry.

Nancy is a contributing editor for the *New York Enterprise Report* and has been published and quoted in *The New York Times*, *Crain's New York*, Smart Money TV, *Businessweek*, Enterpreneur.com, the Associated Press, AOL Small Business, and other media. She serves on the board of Yonkers Partners in Education.

She is the author of two blogs, Hippy to Wiki and theONblog, and two "tip books," *Your Handy Dandy Guide to the Web* and *Your Handy Dandy*

Guide to Trade Shows. She also publishes a line of business comic books called "Bad Girl, Good Business."

She holds an AB in English and psychology from the University of Michigan in Ann Arbor and a graduate diploma in book publishing from New York University. She also completed Kellogg's Executive Communications program at Northwestern University.

Nancy speaks frequently to business groups on a variety of marketing topics, including branding, green marketing, PR, social media, and career development.

She has two daughters and lives in New York. In her spare time, she reads, writes, watches reality TV (yeah, we all have our vices), listens to a variety of loud music, plays with electronic devices, spends way too much time on Facebook (and other forms of social media), knits, bakes, watches movies, and lies slothfully in the sun.

Lindsay E. Brown

Lindsay E. Brown doesn't yet have thirty years of experience doing anything, but she's been told she's wise beyond her years. After working for a while at a reputable advertising agency in Manhattan, she left cubicle farms, the grind of big city life, and the happy hour scene to follow her true passions and relaunch her career. In her new lifestyle, Lindsay began the healing process in recovering from a struggle with an eating disorder, learning to love both herself and the natural world from the inside out. She channeled her new-found positive energy into sustainability, vegetarianism, and healthy living, and she catapulted herself into the media and publishing worlds.

Lindsay is now a popular columnist, consultant, and eco-activist whose writing has appeared in notable media including *Cottages & Gardens* and *Edible East End*. She contributes to EarthHour.org and is a business writer for Thrifty&Green.com; she also pens the interview series Heroines for the Planet on Eco-Chick.com. Lindsay was named in *Ecover's 30*

Americans Under 30, in which the nation's young leaders in environmentalism are recognized for their efforts, and she also organized and led a rally in Central Park for 350.org's Climate Change Day.

Lindsay's a self-professed networking junkie who prides herself on her ability to connect with others, maintain strong relationships, and forge new ones. (That's how she met Nancy!) Lindsay serves as a creative consultant for theONswitch, and she shares her eco-musings and interviews at her blog, brownlovesgreen.com. She's thrilled and humbled by the opportunity to promote healthy living and choices—in and out of work—to women across the country.

She holds a BS in marketing and global business studies from Manhattan College.

Lindsay lives and plays with her dog Layla in New York. In her downtime, she experiments with vegetarian cooking, makes all-natural beauty products (sometimes unsuccessfully), reads nonfiction nightly, gardens, and savors healthy, happy hours at the gym.

How and Where to Find Us

Nancy and Lindsay are available for a wide range of workshops and speaking appearances. Find out more at **www.2booms.com**.

Talk to us! Ask questions on our website's blog and start a conversation. Email us at **nancy@2booms.com** or **lindsay@2booms.com** with your questions, comments, and suggestions...as well as the challenges you'd like to see us address in future 2Booms projects!

Custom imprints, product placement, and special volume discounts are also available for this book. Email us at **info@2booms.com** to learn more.

You can also find out more about The Boss Lady at **www.nunumedia. com** and **www.theonswitch.com**.

And, of course, we're on Facebook, Twitter, and LinkedIn!

The Boss Lady and Lindsay welcome you to . . .

2 B☮⬜MS™

TWO BOOMS

We're closing the digital divide.

No matter what type of pad you work and live in—an iPad or a crash pad—these timeless truths apply. This book is just the first step in closing the generation and communication gaps. Watch for more to come! See our mission statement!

Here are ten truisms from The Boss Lady that live on . . . from the 1960s to the 2000s. Only by talking to each other— with real words, not just texts—can we listen to and learn from each other's perspectives.

1. Legal Stalking

A twenty-something showed up at my client's retail store. She had sent in a résumé but hadn't heard back, so she used her "live" skills to impress. She was offered the job within twenty-four hours—in part because of her ingenuity, resourcefulness, and persistence! Another qualified candidate who didn't return the CEO's call within twenty-four hours lost out, and she may never learn why.

2. Text or Telephone?

If you work with baby boomers, be sure to ask how they prefer to be communicated with! I was just asked by a twenty-something who works for me how I like to receive different types of information. A great question—and one that showed respect for different generations' communication styles.

3. Join the Team!

My best young women employees had played organized sports in high school and college. They respected their teammates and held in-office "cheers" to keep peers motivated. Even if you never lifted a ball, treat your coworkers as if you are all playing on the same field.

4. Show Your Social Media Fabulosity

Your generation has amazing social media skills. Teach your elders what you know—but be patient! Offer your help, but not in a condescending manner.

5. Listen and Study Up

We all still have lots to learn. You may know how to tweet and have amazing innovative ideas. And my generation can provide a wealth of knowledge too. We all need to remember that we can always learn from others. Be sure to keep reading and asking questions. Sites like Mashable will keep you on top of your social media game. And the New York Times and the Wall Street Journal (print or online) are chock-full of business wisdom.

6. Short Shorts or Suit?

Of course you may be more comfortable in a butt-baring mini. And all the young women in your office may wear them. But will your boss take you to that important client meeting if you look like a camp counselor? Dress the part that you want in the future.

7. The Buddy System

If you're tackling a particularly scary project, engage a trusted coworker or mentor to guide you along the way. Just don't become a Siamese twin. Show your independence as you build confidence. One of our interns always took a peer with her to run simple errands (like mailing packages). It looked to me like she was more interested in chitchat than career development.

8. Facts = Power

You may not be a "math girl," but if you can translate information into statistics, you'll build credibility. By quoting relevant and quantifiable facts, you'll immediately seem smarter.

9. Tears and Tantrums

If something or someone at work makes you cry, try to hold it in until you get to the ladies' room or take a walk around the block. Although human emotion is a part of life, your boss wants to know you can hold your temper in check at critical times. Don't whine or blame other people . . . take responsibility for your own happiness.

10. Going Boss-less

Many entrepreneurial twenty-somethings are starting their own ventures right out of college and grad school. That's admirable and bold for sure! But cockiness and an "I know everything" attitude may piss off colleagues, clients, and vendors; beginners need to remember that seasoned entrepreneurs have much to offer. Humility at any age is a valuable trait. Just as you don't like being lectured by baby boomers, we don't like being told we don't know anything. After all, we've lived (and worked) a long time!

Let's all live in peace, love, and prosperity!

The 2BOOMS™ Mission

THROUGH OUR CROSS-GENERATIONAL COLLABORATION
(boomers and "new boomers"), we will help consumers
and businesses by providing practical guidance in a fun,
honest, and sometimes irreverent voice, covering timely
and relevant topics that affect both groups. We will
bridge the generation gap by directly addressing
differences and commonalities in beliefs, behaviors,
communication styles, personal styles, and work ethics.
We will attract like-minded fans to build communities and
networks, leading provocative and dynamic conversations.
We are frank, humorous, a bit naughty, accessible, thoughtful,
helpful, inspirational, wildly creative, fun-loving, and collaborative.

www.ingramcontent.com/pod-product-compliance
Lightning Source LLC
Chambersburg PA
CBHW060801050426
42449CB00008B/1483